Volume 2

# STUDIES IN THE SYNTAX OF RELATIVE AND COMPARATIVE CAUSES

# STUDIES IN THE SYNTAX OF RELATIVE AND COMPARATIVE CAUSES

AVERY D. ANDREWS III

Routledge
Taylor & Francis Group

LONDON AND NEW YORK

First published in 1985 by Garland Publishing, Inc.

This edition first published in 2017
by Routledge
2 Park Square, Milton Park, Abingdon, Oxon OX14 4RN

and by Routledge
711 Third Avenue, New York, NY 10017

*Routledge is an imprint of the Taylor & Francis Group, an informa business*

*British Library Cataloguing in Publication Data*
A catalogue record for this book is available from the British Library

ISBN: 978-1-138-21859-8 (Set)
ISBN: 978-1-315-43729-3 (Set) (ebk)
ISBN: 978-1-138-20776-9 (Volume 2) (hbk)
ISBN: 978-1-315-46117-5 (Volume 2) (ebk)

**Publisher's Note**
The publisher has gone to great lengths to ensure the quality of this reprint but
points out that some imperfections in the original copies may be apparent.

**Disclaimer**
The publisher has made every effort to trace copyright holders and would welcome
correspondence from those they have been unable to trace.

# Studies in the Syntax
# of Relative and Comparative Clauses

Avery D. Andrews III

Garland Publishing, Inc. ■ New York & London
1985

Library of Congress Cataloging-in-Publication Data

Andrews, Avery D. (Avery Delano), 1949–
   Studies in the syntax of relative and comparative clauses.

   (Outstanding dissertations in linguistics)
   Originally presented as the author's thesis (Ph.D.—Massachusetts Institute of Technology), 1975.
   Bibliography: p.
   1. Grammar, Comparative and general—Relative Clauses.   2. Grammar, Comparative and general—Comparative clauses.   3. English language—Comparative clauses.
   I. Title.  II. Series.
   P297.A53  1985     415     85-15903
   ISBN 0-8240-5419-9 (alk. paper)

The volumes in this series are printed on
acid-free, 250-year-life paper.

Printed in the United States of America

To Cindy

## Meditatio

When I carefully consider the curious habits of dogs
I am compelled to conclude
That man is the superior animal.

When I consider the curious habits of man
I confess, my friend, I am puzzled.

--    Ezra Pound

Acknowledgements

I am indebted to many people in the preparation of
this thesis. Susumo Kuno, David Perlmutter and Stephen
Anderson brought me into linguistics, and started me working on many of the topics that now concern me, and have
helped me with discussions on a variety of specific problems
connected with this work.

Ken Hale and Paul Kiparsky, who understand everything that has to do with language, have helped me continu-
ally throughout my time at MIT. Hu Matthews has also
greatly aided my development. Morris Halle and Noam Chomsky,
*che discernono della vera cittade almen la torre*, have
helped with their teaching, advice and encouragement, and
have by example set the highest intellectual standards.
What conception I have of serious work derives largely from
them. Finally, my advisor, Haj Ross, has long listened to
my stories, corrected my papers, and curbed my excesses.
His and Professor Chomsky's extensive remarks on earlier
drafts of this thesis have been enormously valuable.

I have also benefitted from contact with George
Lakoff, Paul Postal and Jim McCawley, who have influenced
my thinking on a variety of topics. I am especially grateful to Joan Bresnan, whose work has provided a basis for
much of my own, and whose advice and encouragement has been
very helpful. Howard Lasnik, J.R. Vergnaud, and Wayles
Browne have also stirred and provoked me with useful stimu-
lation and criticism.

Among past and present fellow students, I would
especially like to thank Mark Liberman, Cindy Allen, Sandy
Chung and Michael Szamosi; and also Arlene Berman, Fred
Katz, Ivan Sag, Dorothy Siegel, Edwin Williams, Bob Fiengo,
Bob May and Jane Grimshaw. Claudia Corum, Polly Jacobson
and Larry Martin deserve a wave of the hand as well.

Needless to say, I, rather than these scholars, am
responsible for the many faults of this work.

I owe a debt to a succession of roommates and
friends who have tolerated more household negligence than
they should have had to, and especially Bob and Michael,

who had to put up with the special chaos of dissertation year.

I would like to thank my parents and family, whose confidence that I would actually get through it all has supported me in many moments of doubt, and also Carey and Edith Welch for their friendship in Cambridge.

I am grateful again to Cindy, for help other than intellectual.

And last, a word for Fran, who as we all know, really runs the department.


\*   \*   \*   \*


I would like to thank Ellalene Seymour for typing this version of the manuscript and Rose Butt for checking it.  This was made possible by the support of the Department of Linguistics, The Faculties, The Australian National University.

# Contents

Introduction...................................... 1

Chapter 1.  A Typology of Relative Clauses.......... 4

   1.1  Constituent Structure Relations............ 10

   1.2  The Treatment of $NP_{rel}$.................... 83

   1.3  The Extraction Analysis.................... 108

   Footnotes to Chapter 1.......................... 114

   Appendix to Chapter 1........................... 116

Chapter 2.  Comparative Clauses in English......... 117

   2.1  The Head, Revisited........................ 118

   2.2  Comparative Clauses in the Base............ 156

   2.3  Global Relations........................... 172

   Footnotes to Chapter 2.......................... 196

Bibliography....................................... 197

# INTRODUCTION

Bresnan (1972) suggested that much of the grammar of
sentence-embedding could be divided into two areas:   the
'predicate complement' system and the 'determiner complement' system.  Predicate complements serve in syntactic
structure as complements to nouns, verbs and adjectives,
and correspond in logical structure to the arguments of
predicates.  Determiner complements are the relative and
comparative clauses.  They appear to bear some sort of
relationship to determiners, and in logical structure, they
restrict the variables bound by the operators corresponding
to these determiners.  In this study, I will pursue two
different approaches towards the syntax of the determiner
complement system.

In chapter one, I conduct a typological survey of relative clauses in the languages of the world.  I direct most
of my attention to determining the varieties of constituent
structure relations between relative clauses and their heads.
I ultimately discern three major types:   headless relatives,
which have no head embedded relatives, which may occur
either attached to their head or extraposed;   and adjoined
relatives, which appear at the beginning or the end of the
matrix.  The distinction between extraposed relatives and
adjoined relatives that follow their matrix will not emerge
until the discussion of adjoined relatives in section 1.1.3.,
and will be further developed in chapter two.

One major finding is that the various types have underlying structures that are largely identical to their surface

structures. Headless relatives lack heads in underlying
structure, and extraposed and adjoined relatives are not
generated as underlying constituents with their heads, but
in their surface positions. I propose that headless relatives are introduced by a rule NP → $\bar{\bar{S}}$, embedded relatives
on heads are introduced by NP → NP $\bar{\bar{S}}$ and NP → $\bar{\bar{S}}$ NP, extraposed relatives are introduced by S → S $\bar{\bar{S}}$, and adjoined
relatives are introduced by $\bar{\bar{S}}$ → COMP ($\bar{\bar{S}}$) S ($\bar{\bar{S}}$). The principal evidence for the claim that extraposed and adjoined
relatives are generated in the base in their surface positions is that they both may have multiple heads.

I also examine various things that happen to the "relative" NP (<u>wh</u> Marking, Deletion, etc.) in the relative
clause, and discuss some possible evidence that the heads
of relative clauses are extracted from within them as a
copy of the relative NP.

In the course of the chapter I discuss numerous theoretical issues, but the primary focus is descriptive and
suggestive rather than theoretical. There are obviously
great limitations on the depth and breadth of the coverage
of individual languages. Furthermore, reduced relatives
will not be treated, and the structures most closely related
to relative clauses, interrogative and focus constructions,
will be ignored. Despite these limitations, I believe that
the chapter provides a valid and useful picture of the relative clause construction in universal grammar.

In chapter 2, I examine comparative clauses in English,
integrating the material with selected aspects of the work
in chapter one, and taking a considerably more theoretical
standpoint. I first examine Bresnan's (1973) analysis of
the head constituents of comparative clauses, such constituents as *as good a linguist* in *he is as good a linguist
as she is*. I modify the analysis in certain respects, and
formulate the crucial rule of 'QP Raising' that Bresnan
leaves unformulated. I also extend the analysis to accomo-
date the 'indefinite comparative' construction of *the more
you study, the less you know*.

In the course of these efforts, I motivate certain

theoretical principles on the basis that they reduce the range of data needed to determine the correct analysis of grammatical phenomena. Some are principles of rule-application to ensure that rules motivated by simple paradigms apply correctly in more complex cases. There is also a convention rendering certain potential derived constituent structures ungrammatical. This rules out an analysis which the evaluation measure prefers for a small data set in favor of a more complex analysis that is in fact the correct one when more data is considered.

The identification of certain analyses as minimal is based on possibly erroneous inspection rather than rigorous proof, and is aided by the assumption, perhaps too strong, that the data which determines the selection of grammars specifies certain strings as ungrammatical, and provides the deep structures for those that are grammatical. Despite the lack of rigour and the overly strong nature of the assumptions, the discussion shows that it is possible to argue from explanatory adequacy with a considerable higher degree of explicitness than is usually attempted (with certain exceptions, such as some recent work by Hamburger, Culicover and Wexler).

Further implications are that Bach's universal rule hypothesis, suggested by Peters (1972) as a solution to the projection problem (the problem of getting linguistic data to determine grammars and thereby project the given data to predictions of more data) may be an unnecessarily violent step. One can get substantial results from imposing highly substantive restrictions on linguistic structure without dictating an inventory of rules. One might, for example, consider a restriction requiring that an S (a) be coordinate (b) be a predicate nominal or adjective construction (c) or otherwise have exactly one verb.

I next show that the traditional assumption that comparative clauses in English are generated in the determiners of the QP they modify cannot be maintained. I show that ordinary comparatives correspond to embedded relatives, being introduced by a rule $X^3 \rightarrow X^3 \bar{S}$ ($N^3$ being, for example,

an X-bar notation for NP) when they appear attached to a
head, and by S → S S̄ when they appear extraposed. I then
show that the indefinite comparative mentioned above corresponds to the adjoined relative clause.

I finally develop, in rather tentative and incomplete
form, a solution to the classical problem of the selection
restrictions between degree particles and complementizers
of comparative and result clauses, and of similar restrictions involving relative clauses and their heads. The
solution takes the form of a system of extra-constituent
structure 'global relations' between degree particles and
NP determiners and the complementizers of relative and
comparative clauses. As much of the theory of this system
as I formulate is common to both comparative and relative
clauses, thus supporting Bresnan's claim that they constitute a unified system, the determiner complement system.

I close by using the mechanisms developed to formulate
some principles that have the effect of reducing the data-
base needed to determine correct analyses for relative
clauses, thus returning to the problem of projection taken
up at the beginning of the chapter.

# 1. THE TYPOLOGY OF RELATIVE CLAUSES:[1]

In this chapter I offer a typological survey of relative
clauses in the languages of the world. The genesis of this
work is the observation of Bach (1965) that relative clauses
differ less between languages than one might expect. It
appears that a limited number of options are being put together in a limited number of ways. The goal of this study
is then to present a broad picture of what relative clauses
are like in the languages of the world.

What is a relative clause? For the purposes of this
chapter, a relative clause is any clause with approximately
the semantic structure and function of a relative clause
(restrictive or nonrestrictive) in English. I shall sharpen
this rough criterion somewhat by saying that a relative
clause is a subordinate clause that modifies a constituent
external to it by virtue of containing a constituent that is

in some sense semantically equivalent to the modified constituent. I shall call the modified constituent the head
constituent, and the equivalent constituent within the
relative clause the relative constituent. In the case
where both are NP, I shall designate them as $NP_{hd}$ and $NP_{rel}$.
The relative clause and its matrix clause I shall designate
as $S_{rel}$ and $S_{mat}$. In addition to being vague, this account
is also too narrow: we shall find in section 1.1.2 a kind
of relative clause that has no head constituent. But in
spite of its deficiencies, this account permits work to
begin.

To improve on my intuitive description of the semantic
structure and function of relative clauses, it would be
necessary to adopt some particular theory of the semantics
of natural languages. I shall not do so here, but refer
the reader to (Keenan 1972), (Montague 1974) and (Hintikka
1974) for some interesting alternatives. On the basis of
the theoretical discussion of relative clauses that I will
offer in chapter two, I will provide a syntactic definition
of the notion 'relative clause.

Once one has made the initial observation that there do
not seem to be terribly many types of relative clause constructions, an attempt to construct a systematic inventory
of relative clause types is immediately justified. To the
extent that there is inexplicably little variation in the
syntactic structures used to express some kind of logical
form, there is a possibility for narrowing linguistic
theory, and therefore for achieving a better explanation of
the possibility of learning languages.

This consideration is strengthened by the fact that the
relative clause is a structure with extremely rich connections elsewhere in the theory of grammar. Some of the more
prominent syntactic contributors are the determiner system
of NP, the grammar of subordinate clauses, pronominalization, syntactic variables, and functional sentence perspec-
tive. On the semantic side, relativization is no less involved with other aspects of grammar, for example with
variables, scope and binding; with coreference, and with

presupposition. Hence, restrictions on relativization are likely to be reflections of more general restrictions of broad explanatory potency.

The primary purpose of this survey is to provide a background of information about diverse languages in order to convey a sense of what relativization is like in the languages of the world. I also wish, however, to suggest a general theory, which I develop gradually and informally in this chapter, and present more formally in the text.

The principal results of the survey are that some relative clauses do not have heads in underlying structure, and that others do not at any level of structure form constituents with their heads, but rather may be separated from them by an unbounded stretch of material. Most theories of relative clauses make crucial use of constituent structure relations between relative clauses and their heads in stating various rules and restrictions. For example, wh-Preposing rules for relative clauses are often given a form like (1):

$$(1) \quad W_1 - [_{NP} \; NP - [_S \; W_2 - NP - W_3]] - W_2, \quad 2 = 4$$

$$\begin{array}{ccccccc} 1 & 2 & 3 & 4 & 5 & 6 & \Longrightarrow \\ 1 & 2 & 4+3 & \emptyset & 5 & 6 & \end{array}$$

To preserve an account of the rules and restrictions involving relative clauses in the face of the breakdown of constant constituent structure relations between relative clauses and their heads, I propose a theory of extra-constituent structure relations that identify the relative and modified constituents of relative clauses. These relations may be represented as systems of directed arrows connecting the nodes of a tree. A more formal treatment will be given in chapter 2.

I develop the theory as an extension of Bresnan's theory of complementizers (Bresnan 1970, 1972, 1974a). Bresnan hypothesizes that clauses are introduced by a rule $\bar{S} \rightarrow COMP \; S$ (or by its trivial variant $\bar{S} \rightarrow S \; COMP$) where COMP is the category of the clause-introductory particles that Bresnan calls complementizers. These complementizers then determine

important aspects of the semantic interpretation of main
and subordinate clauses. Important among the complementizers recognized by Bresnan are the *that* that introduces
many finite clauses, the *for* that introduces infinitives,
the abstract 'Q' that Baker (1968, 1970) proposes to introduce questions and indirect questions, and the *than* and
*as* that introduce comparative (and some relative) clauses.

I propose that universal grammar provides a feature of
COMP, 'R', that is specified as [+R] on the COMP of relative clauses. A preterminal that is [+COMP +R] I shall
call a relative complementizer. 'R' guides semantic interpretation of relative clauses in a language universal
fashion, and is also involved in language particular grammar in various ways. For example, many languages have
special morphemes that precede or follow relative clauses.
These may be regarded as elements that are lexically inserted for relative complementizers.

I shall extend Bresnan's theory by claiming that there
are two extra-constituent structure relations in which
relative complementizers participate. First, there is the
trigger-target relation, which holds between the COMP of a
relative clause and its relative constituent. Second,
there is the head-trigger relation that holds between the
COMP of a relative clause and its head constituent. In
cases where these constituents have determiners, it seems
best to relate the COMP with the determiners rather than
with the containing constituents. The reasons for this will
be seen in chapter 2.

Assuming English relative clauses to be introduced by
an NP → NP S̄ rule, we then get the following representation
for *the boy who Zack gave a joint to*:

(2)

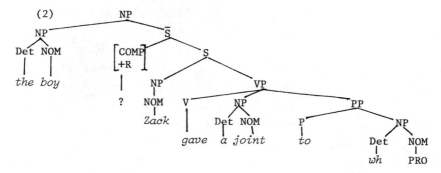

The extra-constituent structure relations are crucially used in explaining the properties of examples in which the relative clause cannot be associated with the head by a simple constituent structure relation. Such an example is Ross and Perlmutter's (1970) *a man came in and a woman went out who were similar:*

(3)

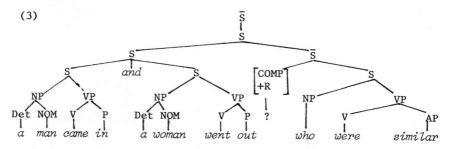

Observe that the nature of the predicate in the relative clause makes it impossible to derive this example by extra-posing the relative clause within each conjunct and then applying Right Node Raising.

The reasons for formulating the system along the lines given here instead of in other ways that one might imagine will be primarily developed in chapter 2. Observe for the present, however, that Baker's (1968, 1969) work on questions (attacked by (Kuno and Robinson 1972) and re-supported by (Hankamer 1974)) shows that there are connections between complementizers and 'target' constituents within their clauses in cases where there is nothing like a head constituent. Furthermore, the properties of result clauses associated with (sometimes multiple) occurrences of *so* in examples like *Bill drank so much beer in so little time that he*

*threw up* (see Liberman 1974)) show that there are connections between clauses and head constituents that are
separated from them even when there is no constituent in
the clause other than the complementizer that can be connected to the head.  Our treatment thus minimizes the
variety of extra-constituent structure relations utilized.

I shall conduct the study under several limitations of
scope.  First, I shall for the most part be restricted to
describing the more obvious formal properties of relative
clauses:  what morphemes mark them, whether anything moves
or deletes, where it goes, etc..  Subtler topics, such as
accessibility (see (Keenan 1972), (Keenan and Comrie 1972)),
will sometimes be treated, but only sporadically.

Second, I shall not attempt to consistently draw fine
distinctions between types of relative clauses.  It is
obvious that the category 'relative clause' in English
alone covers a wide range of different constructions, and
in universal grammar the range can only be wider.  There
are for example restrictive relatives, ordinary nonrestrictives on NP, nonrestrictives in both *which* and *as* on constituents other than NP (*Max squealed, for which he'll die;
Mary is pregnant, as you know*), *whatever*-clausal NP (*I'll
take whatever items I find to my superiors*) and pseudo-
relative comparatives (*he's not the linguist he used to be*).
These types are surely only a beginning.  I believe that a
thorough investigation of the variety of types of relative
clauses in English alone would yield many more species than
I discern in this study for language as a whole.

Amongst all these types, the restrictive relative
clause on a definite head, which has the semantic effect of
forming a definite description from a clause, seems to be
the core relative clause.  Almost all languages (Jakobson
reports Gilyak as an exception) have some equivalent to
this construction, while the representation of the other
types is more sparse.  Portguguese, for example, lacks nonrestrictives that modify S (personal communication of Carlos
Quicoli), while Navajo lacks nonrestrictives entirely.  Japanese and Turkish, on the other hand, make no syntactic

distinction between restrictive and nonrestrictive, using the same structure indifferently for both. It is interesting to observe that speakers of these languages seem to have difficulty in seeing the difference between the two usages. Inasmuch as the restrictive clause on a definite head NP seems to be the most prominent and universally represented variety of relative clause, I shall concentrate on it and mention other types less consistently.

Finally, I shall restrict my attention to relatives that are clauses in surface structure. I shall ignore reduced relatives.

The varieties of relative clause construction submit to classification under a unified scheme. On the other hand, languages seem to select their particular inventory of relative constructions in accordance with no obvious principle. I will therefore organize the typology around the kinds of construction rather than around some classification of the languages.

I will introduce a language at the first point in the discussion where it has something especially significant to offer, at that time giving the necessary background information to render the examples comprehensible. I will then return to any given language as often as necessary in the sequel. In an appendix to this chapter, I provide an index of languages that specifies where in the chapter I give substantial discussion of a language, and what my sources of information on it are.

In section 1.1 I discuss the constituent structure relations obtaining between relative clauses and their heads, in section 1.2 I investigate the fate of the relative constituent, and in section 1.3 I review some phenomena that suggest that some relative clauses have their heads extracted from within them.

1.1 Constituent Structure Relations: In surface structure, relative clauses may appear dominated by an NP within their matrix S, or they may appear at the beginning or the end of the matrix, separated from their head by a stretch of material that is in the general case unbounded. The former kind

I call embedded relatives, the latter, adjoined. Embedded
relatives may appear with a head or without one. If they
have a head, they may precede or follow it. We thus have
three varieties of embedded relative clause. There are
then two types of adjoined relative: anticipatory relatives, which precede their matrix and trailing relatives
which follow. I shall also suggest that there are extraposed relatives in addition to trailing relatives.

These five surface structure types seem to divide naturally into three major families: the headed embedded
relatives, comprising pre- and post-relatives, the headless
relatives, and the adjoined relatives. We will find that
the types within each family, which differ from each other
only in relations of linear order, are closely related.
Nevertheless, it will also become apparent that each position has some peculiarities of its own. Hence the existence
of transformational relations between paired linear order
types is possible, but not entirely unproblematic. We will
however, find arguments that the three major families are
not transformationally derived one from another, but rather
that the deep structures for each family are of roughly the
same form as the surface structures.

In section 1.1.1 I will discuss headed embedded relatives, in section 1.1.2 I will discuss headless relatives,
and in 1.1.3 I will discuss adjoined relatives. Finally,
in 1.1.4 I will make some general remarks.

1.1.1 Embedded Relatives with Heads: These are the most
familiar, although perhaps not the most common, types of
relative clauses. All of the types studied in (Bach 1965),
for example, are in this family. Since embedded relatives
with heads have been studied for so long, there are a great
many proposals in circulation as to what their underlying
structures and derivations are. The majority of these are
conveniently summarized and evaluated in (Stockwell,
Schachter and Partee 1973).

If we take (4) as representing the constituent structure
of the English NP,

(4)

then the most conservative alternatives for the structure
of the restrictive relative in English are given by letting
it be introduced by one of the rules Det → Art S̄,
NOM → NOM S̄, N → N S̄ or NP → NP S̄. Of these, my personal
favorite is NP → NP S̄, and I will assume this rule and its
mirror-image NP → S̄ NP when I give structures for pre- and
post- relative clauses.

(Brame 1968) proposes another analysis in which the
head of the relative clause is extracted from within it as
a copy of the relative constituent, of which a pronominal
copy may be left behind in the form of a relative pronoun.
This analysis is proposed in order to explain the grammaticality of such examples as *the headway (that) we made
pleased our advisor.* *headway* is a noun which is characteristically restricted to being an underlying object of *make*.
Brame's analysis explains the grammaticality of the above
example by providing it with an underlying structure in
which this condition is met.

(Vergnaud 1974) works out for French a version of
Brame's analysis in considerable detail. He gives (pp.81-
84) an argument which shows that if there is an extraction
of the head from the clause, then the extracted constituent
must be an NP, and that if there is not such an extraction,
then the NP → NP S̄ analysis must be chosen over the three
alternatives given above.

The argument may be easily adapted to English. Consider
examples such as the following:

(5) a.  The man and the woman who were related got married.
    b.  An electron and a positron that collided produced a
        shower of gamma rays.
    c.  Any boy and any girl who love each other will buy
        this device.

These examples share with Ross and Perlmutter's extraposed
relative (example 3) the property that the nature of the

predicate prevents the relative clause from reaching its
surface position by being generated in each conjunct and
then being fused and attached to the entire coordinate
structure by Right Node Raising. It is immediate that if
one extracts, one must extract NP rather than a sub-constituent of NP; and that the NP → NP $\bar{S}$ analysis can generate
the constituent structure of these examples while the
Det → Art $\bar{S}$, NOM → NOM $\bar{S}$ and N → N $\bar{S}$ analyses cannot.
Although I will not adopt the extraction analysis in the
following pages, in section 1.3 I will discuss a variety
of phenomena which could probably be made to support it.

Although I adopt the NP → NP $\bar{S}$ analysis for post-
relative restrictives and its mirror image for pre-relatives, we shall in the following pages find some difficulties with these rules. One such problem is provided by
examples like *the motion that we made to expel Harry* or *the
proof that I gave in class that pi is irrational* (pointed
out to me by Mark Baltin). If one believes that complement
clauses are introduced by a NOM → N $\bar{S}$ rule, then these
examples suggest that at least some relative clauses are
introduced by an N → N $\bar{S}$ rule. We shall find other such
problems below.

One matter deserving discussion is the constituent
structure of nonrestrictive relatives in English. Unlike
restrictive clauses, nonrestrictives cannot stack:

(6) a. the man who was laughing who you pointed out
        to me was arrested.
    b. *Bill, who was laughing, who you pointed out
        to me, was arrested.

We also observe that a nonrestrictive can be attached to an
NP modified by a restrictive:

(7) the man who was laughing, who you pointed out to me,
    to me, was arrested.

For a restrictive to modify an NP + nonrestrictive combination is, of course, impossible.

Martin (1972), in an extensive study of the restrictive-
nonrestrictive distinction in English, proposes that there
should be as little structural differentiation between the

types as possible, with the major burden of explanation for the distinctions resting upon the differing logical form of the types. But we shall see that in Japanese semantically nonrestrictive clauses seem to be indistinguishable from restrictives, even having the power to stack. This suggests that the special features of nonrestrictives in English should receive an explanation in terms of syntactic structure.

A traditional proposal for the derivation of nonrestrictive relatives is to get them from underlying coordinate structures: a rule called Swooping would produce (8b) from (8a), then nonrestrictive clause formation would yield (8c) from (8b):

(8) a. Clarence is a swinger and he is wearing mauve socks.
b. Clarence, and he is a swinger, is wearing mauve socks.
c. Clarence, who is a swinger, is wearing mauve socks.

(Ross 1967: section 6.2.4.2) notes a difficulty with this derivation:

(9) Is even Clarence, who is a swinger, wearing mauve socks?

Of course we can also embed nonrestrictives in imperatives, and (Martin 1972) notes that imperatives can serve as nonrestrictives within declaratives. Likewise even interrogatives have a marginal capacity to be nonrestrictive relatives. These points are illustrated in the following:

(10) a. Get Bill, who is in charge of this operation.
b. I have included a CV, which find enclosed.
c. I want to talk to that man, who the hell is he, anyway?
d. Thoughts, which how found they harbour in thy breast, / Adam, misthought of her to thee so dear? (Paradise Lost IX 288-289)

Since imperative and interrogative clauses cannot be conjoined with declaratives, the coordinate structure source for nonrestrictive relatives has a problem.

It is interesting to note that 'Swooped' coordinate structures are restricted in the same way that ordinary coordinate structures are:

(11) a. *Is Clarence, and he is a swinger, wearing mauve socks?

    b.  *Buy Clarence, and he is a swinger, a new gas furnace.

This observation reinforces Ross' counterargument to the Swooping derivation for nonrestrictive relatives.

    Ross unenthusiastically proposes to analyse nonrestrictives by resurrecting the concept of 'generalized transformation,' having nonrestrictives derived by a transformation that combines two main clauses. Hence (9) would be derived from (12):

    (12)  Clarence is a swinger. Is even Clarence wearing
           white socks?

(I have reversed the order of clauses from Ross' in order to make the discourse sound better).

    But even this proposal, which Lakoff (1974) has recently advocated generalizing into a theory of 'syntactic amalgams' falls in the face of the following example:[2]

    (13)  everybody got a pen, with which he wrote a letter.

The relative clause here has the superficial appearance of a nonrestrictive, and seems to the intuition to be nonrestrictive in force. Nevertheless, it manages to be within the scope of the universal quantifier in its matrix, as is betrayed by the fact that *he* is bound by that quantifier. Such binding is of course impossible between conjuncts or between main clauses in a discourse:

    (14)  a.  *Everybody got a pen (,) and he wrote a letter
              with it.
          b.  *Everybody got a pen. he wrote a letter with it.

The subordinate clause of (13) also has deeper properties of nonrestrictives. For example, Martin (1972) notes that the relative pronoun of a nonrestrictive, but not of a restrictive, can be the object of *of* in a partitive quantificational construction:

    (15)  a.  The boys, some of whom were rich kids, were arrested.
          b. *The boys some of whom were rich kids were arrested.

Now observe (16):

    (16)  everybody got three pens, with one of which he wrote a
           letter.

Ross' proposal likewise seems doomed.

Chomsky has proposed (class lectures, Spring 1973) to introduce nonrestrictive relatives by a 'three-dimensional' rule NP $\cdots \rightarrow \bar{S}$. This notation means that the relative clause is in the sentence structure and somehow related to the NP it modifies, but does not bear linear order or dominance relations to it. Late linearization rules are then supposed to put the clause in the position where we see it on the surface. This proposal could probably be made to avoid the difficulties we have posted against the others, but it possesses the theoretical demerit of requiring an unworked out and ad-hoc modification in our conception of what a sentence structure is. A proposal within the bounds of ordinary notions of constituent structure would be preferable.

Work by Siegel (1974) suggests an answer. Siegel proposes that NP in English (and in languages generally) are introduced by a rule CP → NP CASE (or, of course, its mirror image). She identifies CP as N and NP as N, but this is irrelevant here. We may explain the facts that nonrestrictives do not stack and that they follow restrictives by introducing them as sisters of NP under CP. The following examples show that nonrestrictives cannot follow the genitive case-marker:

(17)  a.  *Bill's, who is a swinger, house is too cold.
      b.  *I gave a picture of Bill's, who is a swinger,
             to Maurice.

I therefore propose to introduce nonrestrictive relatives by revising Siegel's rule to CP → NP ($\bar{S}$) CASE.

We may also observe that nonrestrictives do not sound very good before the genitive case-marker:

(18)  a.  ? *Bill, who is a swinger, 's house is too cold.
      b.  ? *I gave a picture of Bill, who is a swinger, 's
             to Maurice.

This may be explained by the observation that the genitive case-marker 's is an element which must be a phonological word with the material immediately preceding it. The pause that follows nonrestrictives makes this impossible.

I shall return to the subject of nonrestrictive relatives and Swooping in chapter 2.  For the present, I shall
end by calling attention to two of the most obvious questions of universal grammar that are raised by my proposal.
First, is the association of NP → NP S̄ with restrictive and
CP → NP (S̄) CASE with nonrestrictive relativization an
accident of English?  Second, what linear order variants
does the CP → NP (S̄) CASE rule have?  I do not have answers
to these questions, though I will venture a speculation in
section 1.1.1.4.

Now, at last, on to the long-awaited languages!  In
section 1.1.1.1 I will look at post-relative clauses, in
1.1.1.2 I will look at pre-relatives and in 1.1.1.3 I will
examine a number of languages in which the two constructions cooccur.  The main result to emerge will be that
these relative clauses are the same as adjectives in their
external constituent structure relations.  Finally, in
1.1.1.4 I will summarize the results and speculate on some
tendencies associated with linear order of head and relative clause.

1.1.1.1  Post-Relatives:  I have proposed two underlying
structures for post-relative clauses in English, (19) for
restrictives, and (20) for nonrestrictives:

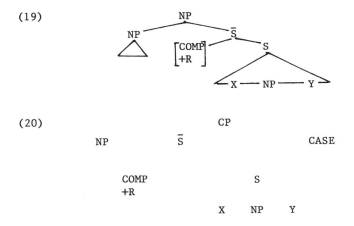

(19)

(20)

Some languages with a post-relative clause construction
that are genetically unrelated are the following:

(21) Languages having Post-relative Clauses:

| | |
|---|---|
| English | Samoan |
| Hungarian | Maasai |
| Hebrew | Micmac |
| Georgian | Eskimo |
| Swahili | Shan |
| Nuer | Vietnamese |
| Crow | Dyirbal |
| Papago | Dagbani |
| Hottentot | |

It requires subtle work to choose between (19) and (20), or to argue for them against alternatives. I shall not, therefore so decide for the languages I examine. We will find the evidence consistent with either of the alternatives.

I shall look first at Samoan, then at Faroese, and finally at Eskimo.

1.1.1.1.1 *Samoan*[3]: Samoan is a VSO language. Naturally then, most modifiers of NP follow the head: adjectives, non-pronominal possessive phrases, prepositional phrases and relative clauses. $S_{rel}$ may have $NP_{rel}$ present in surface structure as a pronoun, or, in subject or object position, the pronoun may be deleted by regular processes of anaphoric pronoun deletion.

Here we see adjectives and possessives following the head N:

(22)  a.  'o  le  teine puta
          Prt. the girl  fat
          "the fat girl"

      b.  'o  va'a  lapopo'a
          Prt. boats big
          "big boats"

      c.  'o le  paopao o  Tavita
              the canoe of David
          "the canoe of David"

      d.  'o le  naifi a  le  taule'ale'a
              the knife of the young man
          "the knife of the young man"

The particle *'o* precedes NP in a variety of environments which I do not understand. One of them is when the NP is being cited. The choice between *a* and *o* is made on semantic grounds which are quite obscure, even to student of Polynesian.

These examples show relative clauses that follow the head:

(23) a. 'ua nofo mai i le malō    le tupu fou na te    le'i
PERF come    to the throne the king new he PAST not
iloa 'Iosefa
know Joseph
"There came to the throne a new king who did not know Joseph."

b. 'o i       tangata toa    'ua āva         'iate 'ilātou
there are men    valiant PERF do honor to    them
lea tupulanga ma lea tupulanga
generation after generation
"There are valiant men to whom generation after generation do honor."

c. 'o le mea    lenei 'ua    'ou 'aumaia 'iate 'oe
Prt. the thing this PERF I    bring    to    you
"This is the thing which I bring to you."
(Note that extraposition applies here.)

d. 'ua fa'apea          le tangata 'ua fai masani
PERF is the    same with the man    PERF does habits
leanga
bad
"It is the same with the man who indulges in bad habits."

In all of these examples, $NP_{rel}$ vanishes from the surface form of the relative clause. (24) shows that this can be effected by a rule applying to ordinary anaphoric pronouns:

(24) a. 'ua 'ou 'aumai 'iate 'oe
PERF I    bring to    you
"I have brought it to you."

b. 'ua fai masani leanga
PERF does habits bad
"He indulges in bad habits."

In (25) I give relative clauses in which the relative constituent is a pronominal adverbs, and in (26) I give the corresponding main clauses. The pronominal adverbs are *ai* and *a'i*, which always migrate to behind the verb:

(25) a. 'o tupe 'ua lātou fa'atau a'i    le fanua
Prt. money PERF they buy    with it the field
"the money with which they bought the field"

b. 'o le fale 'u tupu    ai    Moses
Prt. the house PAST grow up in it Moses
"the house which Moses grew up in"

(26)  a.  'ua lātou fa'atau a'i    le fanua
          PERF they  buy      with it the field
          "They bought the field with it."

      b.  'ua tupu    ai
          PAST grew up in it

Grinder (19  ) has observed that Samoan is quite lax
in its observance of Island Constraints.  Perlmutter (1972)
has proposed to explain this on the basis that there is in
Samoan no special rule deleting $NP_{rel}$.  Rather, the efface-
ment, when accomplished at all, is accomplished by Pronoun-
Drop rules that apply generally to anaphoric pronouns.
Pronoun Drop would involve no variables and hence would not
set off Island Constraints.

We may also observe that relative clauses occupy roughly the same position as adjectives, except that they may
appear extraposed (23c).

1.1.1.1.2 *Faroese*:  Faroese is a close relative of Icelandic spoken in the Faroe Islands.  Its conventional
orthography, which I use here, maximizes the resemblance
to Icelandic and minimizes the relation to the surface
phonetic form.

Faroese relative clauses are introduced by Ø, the
particle *sum*, or sometimes by *ið*, and $NP_{rel}$ is deleted.
Like Icelandic, Faroese often suffixes the definite article
of an NP to the head.  When a Faroese definite NP (usually
with the definite article suffixed) has either a relative
clause or an adjective, the demonstrative pronoun *tann*
'that' is usually put before the NP as well.  Hence we find
the following:

(27)  a.  tann svarti kettlingur-inn
          that black  kitten-the
          "the black kitten"

      b.  ta  góða korn-i
          that good corn-the
          "the good corn"

      c.  tey   hægstu fjøll-ini
          those highest mountains-the
          "the highest mountains"

(28) a. tann maður-inn, sum gj∮rdi hettar
         that man-the    that did  this
         "the man who did this"

     b. tað er tað ljótasta      djór, eg nakranti havi soeð
        that is that most loathsome animal I ever    have seen
        "That is the most loathsome animal that I ever have seen."

     c. tær    konur-nar heima    skuldu verða, eru burtursaddar
        those women-the at home should be     are away
        "the women who should be at home are away."

Note that in (28b) the suffixed article is omitted.  I do
not know when this can happen.

These examples show the relative clause acting like an
adjective in a more subtle way than merely being in approximately the same place:  in fact, the adjective and the
relative clause are in different places in the surface
structure.  We shall in 1.1.1.4 adduce a consideration that
suggests that if there is a transformational relationship,
then the position of the relative clause after the head is
the basic one, with adjectives being transformationally
preposed.

1.1.1.3 *Eskimo*[4]:  In Eskimo, the relative clause again has
much the same external constituent structure as does the
adjective, and can in addition be seen to occupy a position
between CASE and the head N.

To render the examples more intelligible, I will present
a thumbnail sketch of Eskimo morphology and syntax.  Eskimo
verbs and nouns are built up from a base morph by adding
first derivational suffixes and then inflectional endings.
The derivational suffixes are many, and the derivational
processes are astonishingly productive, and recursive.
Suffixes have the semantic effect of modifying adjectives
or adverbs, of higher verbs or nouns, or of many other
things.

For example, given a form *X* we may add the suffix *liur*
'to construct,' to get a verb stem meaning 'to construct an
*X*.'  To this may be added another suffix *vig* to get a noun-
stem *X-liur-vig* 'a place in which to construct an *X*.'  After
some more suffixes have been added, perhaps, we may add
*liur* again in order to get a verb meaning 'to construct a

place in which to construct an X.'.

Nouns are inflected for number and case, and have in
addition an agreement suffix showing the person and number
of the possessor, if there is one.  The numbers are singular, dual and plural.  The cases divide naturally into
'syntactic' and 'adverbial.'  The syntactic cases are the
relative and the absolutive.  The relative case is used on
possessors of NP and on subjects of transitive verbs.  It
is thus a genitive-ergative (a great deal of Eskimo scho-
larship has been devoted to trying to make this dual function of the relative follow from something).  It is marked
with a suffix that is underlyingly a labial, appearing on
the surface mostly as *p* or *m*.  The absolutive case is used
on the subjects of intransitive verbs and the objects of
transitives, and is not marked by any formative.  Thus it
consists of the stem alone.  The adverbial cases are Instrumental, Locative, Allative, etc., and appear to be marked
by suffixes that are attached to the relative case-form of
the noun.

The basic order of elements of the NP is *(Possessor)*
*Head* $\binom{Adjective}{Relative\ Clause}$.  Adjectives are morphologically
indistinguishable from nouns.  It is not clear that they
are even a separate class of stems.  They agree with the
head in number and case.  Adjectives must be distinguished
from a class of adjectival suffixes that may be added to
any nominal stem.

Verbs have a mood suffix followed by subject and object
agreement suffixes.  Furthermore, stems (which are structures of the form *Base + one or more Derivational Suffixes)*
are almost always inherently transitive or intransitive,
with inherently transitive stems being understood as reflexive when they appear with intransitive inflection.  The
moods are various, including an indicative, which is used
in declarative main clauses, which has the mood suffix *-va*
when transitive and *-vu* when intransitive, an interrogative
for questions, transitive and intransitive participial
moods, which appear to be nominalization forms of verbs,
and various others.

The syntax of relative clauses with transitive verbs is exceedingly complex and difficult to discern, owing to the paucity of examples and multiplicity of structures that they seem to exhibit. But relative clauses with intransitive verbs are comparatively straightforward. They are formed by putting the main verb of $S_{rel}$ into the intransitive participial mood and deleting $NP_{rel}$.

The intransitive participial appears to be the form which nominalized intransitive verbs normally take. Hence we have (29):

> (29) passi-ssa-v-r-put       ... kalaaliy-u-šu-gut
> realize-FUT-TR.IND-it-we     Greenlander-be-INT.PRT-we
> "We shall realize that we are Greenlanders."
> (Bergsland 29.4, pg. 46)

(All examples are from (Bergsland 1955), and the transcription used is his). TR.IND is the hieratic symbol for the transitive indicative mood marker, and INT.PRT is that for the intransitive participial. Here *kalaaliušugut* 'we being Greenlanders' is the object of *paasissavarput* 'we shall realize it.' *r* in the main verb is the agreement suffix referencing the nominalized S.

In relative clauses, if $NP_{rel}$ is the subject of $S_{rel}$, then it is deleted, and the intransitive participial acts pretty much like an ordinary adjective. An example of this is (30):

> (30) iglu-ni           tammar-tu-q           uyar-i-ni
> cousin$_j$-his$_i$ be lost-INT.PRT-he$_j$ see-TR.PRT-him$_j$-he$_i$
> his$_i$ cousin$_j$ who$_j$ was lost    he$_i$ seeking him$_j$
>
> unnir-lu-gu
> say-CONT-him$_j$
>
> saying of him$_j$
> "Saying that he$_i$ was looking for his$_i$ cousin$_j$ who$_j$ was lost
> (Bergsland 29.5.2, pg. 46)

CONT is the symbol for one of the subordinate verbal moods which is used mostly when the time of the subordinate clause is roughly the same as that of the matrix clause, and the subjects of both are identical. If the CONT verb is transitive, as it is here, then its own subject is deleted and leaves no agreement marker on the verb.

*ni* in *igluni* 'his cousin' and *uyarini* 'he seeking him'
is the agreement suffix of the so-called fourth person.
This is really a kind of reflexive pronoun, used when the
antecedent asymmetrically commands (with respect to both
S and NP nodes) the pronoun, and the antecedent is a subject. This reflexivization process is not clause-bounded.
The pronoun is virtually always deleted by normal anaphoric
processes, leaving the fourth person suffix as a remnant.
In *uyarini*, the TR.PRT ending is phonologically reduced and
the object agreement suffix is destroyed.

More interesting are some examples in which $NP_{rel}$ is
the possessor of the subject of $S_{rel}$. The verbal character of the intransitive participial verb of $S_{rel}$ is shown
by its taking a subject in the absolutive case, regardless
of the case of $NP_{hd}$. Bergsland claims that the participial
agrees in number with its subject and in case with the $NP_{hd}$.
Unfortunately, in the examples he gives, the head and the
subject of $S_{rel}$ are identical in number.

(31)  a.  natsir-niq          miqquw-i
          seal skin-PL.INSTR hair-PL their
          with seal skins     their hairs
             qummu-kar-tu-nik
             upwards-go-INT.PRT-PL.INSTR
             they going upwards
          "with seal skins whose hairs go upwards"
          (Bergsland 19.3, pg.45)

      b.  ukiyuliguni          nanu-ršu-up
                               bear-big-REL(case)
          when winter comes big bear
             kiina-a  miqqu-qu-ŋŋitšur-su-up
             face-its hair-have-not-INTR.PRT-it REL(case)
             its face it having no hair (the face)
                tikiraa-qqip-pa-si
                come (visiting)-again-IRREAL-it you
                it comes visiting you again
          "When winter comes, when the big polar bear whose
             face has no hair again comes to you."
          (Bergsland 1971.2, pg.49)

IRREAL is the symbol for the Irrealis mood, used in
various subordinate clauses referring to things that haven't
happened yet. In each example there is a subject of $S_{rel}$,
and this subject is absolutive in case. The verb is $S_{rel}$,
which is an intransitive participial, sports the case end-

ing of NP$_{hd}$, just as an adjective would.  In these examples,
as well as in the previous ones, NP$_{rel}$ disappears.  It is
clear that in the above examples it is not NP$_{hd}$ which is
disappearing, because if NP$_{rel}$ were to survive it would be
absolutive in case.  This disappearance can be taken as a
consequence of the Eskimo Pronoun Drop rule:  there is no
need to postulate a special rule which deletes NP$_{rel}$.

There are two arguments afforded by Eskimo concerning
the constituent structure of relative clauses.  First,
since the verb of S$_{rel}$ is nominalized, S$_{rel}$ must be dominated by NP, and, second, since it agrees with NP$_{hd}$ in case,
it is in the same NP as NP$_{hd}$ and is furthermore roughly the
same kind of modifier that an adjective is.  This paralellism is reinforced by the fact that relative clauses and
adjectives are similar in following the head N, whereas
possessors precede it.  We may finally observe that if the
adjectives and relative clauses precede CASE in underlying
structure, the rule case-marking the elements of the NP
(or CP) will be a rule copying case to the left, rather
than a rule spreading it in both directions.  One might
take the NP → NP S̄ analysis as being slightly favored,
because the rule could then be taken as copying the CASE
onto all the major constituents of the NP that follow the
head N except possessives.  These considerations, of course,
are highly tenuous.

1.1.1.2  Pre-Relatives:  For pre-relatives I propose underlying structures of the form given in (32):

(32)

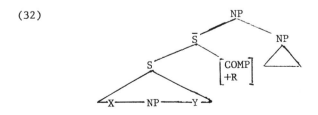

I have found no reason to propose a pre-relative counterpart to (2), the structure produced by the CP → NP (S̄) CASE

rule.  But I do not believe that my research has been suf-
ficent to settle the point.

Below I list some genetically unrelated languages having a pre-relative construction:

(33) Japanese      Korean
     Hottentot     Mongolian
     Turkish       Telugu
     Ainu          Basque
     Navajo        Chinese
     Papago        Classical Tibetan

As representatives of these languages I will discuss Japanese and Turkish.

Before discussing these languages, however, I wish to
venture a brief remark on the structure (32).  The reader
will observe that I have placed the COMP after its S,
rather than before.  This is because I am aware of no pre-
relative clause constructions with introductory particles.
Another fact, however, renders the analysis or clause-final
relative clause markers (such as we shall see in Turkish,
section 1.1.1.2.1.) slightly problematical in individual
languages.  Kuno (1974) has observed that pre-relatives are
characteristic of SOV languages and post-relatives of SVO
and VSO languages.  Therefore, the COMP at the end of a
relative clause may either be a COMP or something inside
the S:  an AUX or an affix on the verb.  I believe that
both situations arise.

1.1.1.2.2 *Japanese*:[4]  The general form of relativization
in Japanese is familiar to linguistics.  See, for example,
the general discussions in (Kuno 1973) and (McCawley 1972),
and the references cited in these works.  In this discussion I intend to make an assortment of points connected
with theoretical issues in this paper:  the constituent
structure of relative clauses, the restrictive/nonrestric-
tive distinction, and the general treatment of $NP_{rel}$.

Japanese is an SOV language with postpositions, conjunctions that follow their sentences, and modifiers,
including relative clauses, that precede what they modify.
Grammatical relations are marked by particles that follow
the NP.

There is a thematic construction in which an NP is placed initial to the S and followed by the particle *wa*, which sometimes follows, and sometimes replaces the particle appropriate to the grammatical relation of the theme NP to the sentence. This construction bears an intimate relation to the grammar of relativization, which is discussed in the above-mentioned work and will also be treated in section 1.3.1 of the present paper. Case-marking and Thematization are discussed in considerable detail in (Kuno 1973), so there is no need to discuss them here.

A relative clause precedes its head, and in the usual construction NP$_{rel}$ vanishes, taking along its postnominal particles. These points I illustrate in (34-35). (34) is a clause embedded in (35a) by relativizing on the object, and in (35b) by relativizing on the subject:

(34)  ano  hito  ga  hon  o  kai-ta
      that person SUBJ book OBJ write-PAST
      "That person wrote a book."

(35)  a.  kore wa    ano hito  ga  kai-ta    hon  desu
          this THEME that person SUBJ write-PAST book is
          "This is a/the book which that person has written."

      b.  kore wa       o  kai-ta    hito  desu
          this THEME book OBJ write-PAST person is
          "This is a/the person who has written a book."

The subject of a relative clause (or other subordinate clause immediately dominated by NP) may be marked with *no*, the possessive or genitive marker, instead of *ga*. Hence (35a) may be rendered *kore wa ano hito no kaita hon desu*.

The first question I will address is the possibility of replicating in a pre-relative structure the argument of Vergnaud (1974) (discussed above in section 1.1.1.) that English and French have a [$_{NP}$ NP $\bar{S}$] surface structure for relative clauses.

While Japanese lacks definite or indefinite articles, it does have the demonstrative pronouns and adjectives *kono* 'this,' *sono* 'that (by you),' and *ano* 'that (yonder).' If we assume that Japanese introduces the demonstratives under the Det produced by an NP → Det NOM rule, then the following example serves to yield a counterpart to Vergnaud's argument.

(36)  otagaini   ai   site  iru ano  otoko  to   ano  onna  ga
      each other love doing be that man  and  that woman SUBJ
      kekon     si-ta
      marriage  do-PAST
      "The man and the woman who loved each other got married."

Unfortunately the claim that relative clauses are introduced by NP → S̄ NP and demonstratives by NP → Det NOM cannot be accepted without further scrutiny. Relative clauses are perhaps best when they precede the demonstrative, but may also come between a demonstrative and its head. These possibilities are shown in (37):

(37)  a.  boku ga    sonkeisite iru kono hito   ga   Tokyo ni
          I    SUBJ respecting be  this person SUBJ Tokyo in
          sunde  iru
          living is

      b.  kono, boku ga sonkeisite iru hito ga Tokyo ni sunde iru
          "That person who I respect lives in Tokyo."

These two possibilities are not quite in free variation, but I do not understand the factors that condition them.

One way to accommodate (36-37) would be to claim that the demonstratives were introduced by a rule NP → Dem NP parallel to the rule introducing relatives. This would require finding some further mechanism to block *ano kono hito*, *kono kono hito*, etc.

I leave the resolution of the questions raised by this discussion to scholars of Japanese. It suffices to point out that a clarification of the constituent structure relations of demonstrative adjectives in Japanese would shed light on the constituent structure relations of relative clauses.

It has often been observed that Japanese does not mark a distinction between restrictive and nonrestrictive relatives. Kuno (1973 pg. 235) cites the following pairings of restrictive and nonrestrictive clauses in order to show the formal indistinctness of the two types:

(38)  a.  watakusi ni eigo     o    osiete    iru Mary
          I        to English OBJ teaching be  Mary
          "Mary, who is teaching me English" (nonrestrictive)

      b.  watakusi ga   sitte   iru Mary
           I        SUBJ knowing be  Mary
           "the Mary that I know" (restrictive)

(39)  a.  honyuu-doobutu de aru kuzira
           mammal        is     whale
           "the whale, which is a mammal" (nonrestrictive)

      b.  nihon-kai ni sunde  iru kuzira
           Japan-sea in living be  whale
           "the whales that live in the Japan sea" (nonrestrictive)

Similarly, Japanese speakers report considerable difficulty in distinguishing between the two types of clauses, which suggests more strongly that Japanese has no syntactic differentiation between the two types.

To confirm these impressions, we find that Japanese nonrestrictive clauses can stack, just as restrictives can:

(40)  kinoo     Mary ga   at-ta,    ringo ga  suki  na    John
      yesterday Mary SUBJ meet-PAST apples SUBJ liking being John
      "*John, who Mary met yesterday, who likes apples"

These clauses in (40) cannot be conjoined, because Japanese does not conjoin clauses by juxtaposition, but requires special final particles on the initial clause.

The fact that Japanese has nonrestrictives that are essentially indistinguishable from restrictives provides the major motivation for providing the two clause types with different syntactic structures in English, inasmuch as this is the most straightforward way to connect the syntactic differences to the semantic.

The final topic I wish to discuss is the treatment of $NP_{rel}$. Kuno (1973) shows that Japanese is quite lax in its obedience to island constraints, as is Samoan. Likewise, Japanese has a very general rule deleting pronouns, even first and second person pronouns. Hence there is no need to postulate for Japanese any special processes deleting $NP_{rel}$: a pronominal $NP_{rel}$ will delete of its own accord by the general rule. To strengthen the plausibility of this explanation, we may observe that Japanese needn't in general delete $NP_{rel}$: it may attain the surface as a pronoun, a demonstrative, or even as a full NP. Kuno (1973 pg. 237) cites the following examples:

```
(41)  watakusi ga    so      kare    sono hito    no    namae o
      I        SUBJ  (that / he   / that person)  POSS  name   OBJ
      wasurete-simat-ta okyaku-san
      forget-PAST        guest
      "the guest whose name I have forgotten"
```

I shall later develop the notion that the presence of such
structures with overt $NP_{rel}$ is related to laxity of island
constraints in languages with very general pronoun deletion
processes.

I here end my discussion of Japanese.

1.1.1.2.2 *Turkish*: Turkish has both pre- and post-relatives.  The post-relatives were borrowed from Persian, and
are apparently frowned upon and disappearing from the
language.  The pre-relatives are the native construction.
Here I shall consider only the pre-relatives, deferring the
post-relatives for 1.1.1.3.1.

Turkish is an SOV language with considerable scrambling
of major constituents in main clauses.  In the noun phrase,
modifiers typically precede the head, with the exception of
the post-relative clause borrowed from Persian.  Turkish
has postpositions and case-markers that follow the head,
marking nominative, accusative, genitive, locative, dative
and ablative cases.  Verbs and nouns have agreement suffixes
referring to their subjects and possessors, respectively.
The suffixes manifest person and number.  Subject and possessor pronouns are freely deletable.  There is considerable
syntactic paralellism between the subject of an S and the
possessor of an NP, since when an S is nominalized, its
subject becomes genitive, and possessor-agreement suffixes
are attached to the nominalized verb.  The subject and
possessor agreement suffixes are morphologically similar,
and were originally identical.

The relative clauses (both pre- and post-) are closely
related to nominalizations corresponding to the English *that*
clauses used as the objects of verbs meaning 'think,' 'say,'
etc.  The post-relative clause is related to a nominal
clause that was borrowed from the Persian along with the
relative.  The pre-relative is related to a native nominalization.

I shall first describe the native nominalization. This is formed with the aid of the 'personal participle' endings. These endings come in two forms: *acak/ecek* (varying by vowel harmony) for the future, and *dig/dig/dug/düg* (again varying by vowel harmony) for the non-future (present and past). These endings replace endings marking a post-non-past distinction in 'finite' clauses, and do not have the possibilities for aspectual elaboration that verbs in finite clauses have. To the personal participle endings are attached possessor agreement suffixes which show the person and number of the subject, which appears in the genitive case. If the nominalized sentence is being used as a direct object, an accusative case marker appears after the agreement suffix, in accordance with the normal rule.

Hence we have examples such as the following:

(42)  a.  Halil Orhan-in  Istambul-a   git-tĭg-i-ni    düsün-üyor
          Halil Orhan-GEN Istambul-DAT go-NOM-his-ACC think-PROG
          "Halil thinks that Orhan went (or is going) to Istambul."

      b.  Hasan, Fatma-nin o-nu    öl-dür-eceğ-i-ni       düsün-üyor
          Hasan  Fatma-GEN he-ACC die-cause-FUT-his-ACC think-PROG
          "Hasan thinks that Fatma will kill him."

A likely explanation for the properties of these nominalizations is that they lack an S node to dominate them in the later stages of the derivation, due to some sort of pruning, or that their S nodes are heavily infused with nominal features. The resulting structure would then be roughly like (43):

(43)

Since the subject NP bears the same structural relation the dominating NP as would a possessor NP, it gets the genitive case. Since the NP and the VP are related in the same way as are a possessor and a possessed NOM, possessor agreement suffixes get copied onto the latter. I assume the VP to be a VP because it has the full range of internal structure of a VP; the full set of complements, adverbs, etc. Siegel (1974) gives a fairly similar analysis of the gerund in English. It is worth pointing out one fact, how-

ever, which is that there is a general dearth of evidence
for a VP node in Turkish. Hankamer (1971) cites the
absence of any pronominal VP comparable to the English *do
so*, and various other sorts of missing possible evidence as
well.

There are two kinds of nonfinite relative clauses: one
where $NP_{rel}$ is within the subject, either as the subject
itself or as its possessor, or even as the possessor of the
possessor, etc.; and the other when $NP_{rel}$ is outside the
subject (that is, in the VP). This latter construction has
the same internal syntax and morphology as do the nominalizations described above, except that $NP_{rel}$ is always deleted (although agreement markers cross-referencing it may
survive). Below are examples:

    (44)  a.  Halil-in  (\*o-nu)  öldür-düǧ-ü adam
                Halil-GEN (him-ACC kill-NOM-his man
                "the man whom Halil killed"

         b.  gel-dik-leri   vapur
                come-NOM-their steamer
                "the steamer on which they came"

         c.  baba-si-nin    ev-i-ni       al-diǧ-imiz adam
                father-his-GEN house-his-ACC buy-NOM-our  man
                "the man whose father's house we bought"

         d.  iç-in-den       cik-tiǧimiz       ev
                interior-its-ABL emerge-NOM-our house house
                "the house from which we emerged"

That there is a deletion rule is demonstrated by (40a-
b) where a pronoun for $NP_{rel}$ results in unacceptability
(contrast with (42)). In (44c-d) it could be that $NP_{rel}$
was being deleted by the rule that deletes unemphatic
subject and possessor pronouns. Object pronouns, however,
do not freely delete, so this account does not extend to
(44a-b).

The other nonfinite construction is used when $NP_{rel}$ is
within the subject. For this form a participle ending
*en/an* is used for nonfuture tense, and the future tense and
a past tense for events not known through personal observation may be expressed with the periphrastic forms *ecek (olan)*
and *miş (olan)* respectively. *olan* in these forms is the *en-*

participial form of the verb *ol* 'to be, become.' The subject of S$_{rel}$ is nominative, and there are no agreement
suffixes on the verb.    Some examples are:

(45)   a.   dün        gel-miş    ol-an   mektup
            yesterday come-PAST be-PRT letter
            "the letter which came yesterday"

       b.   baba-s     şimdi konuş-an  adam
            father-his now   speak-PRT man
            "the man whose father is now speaking"

       c.   oğl-u-nun  kedi-si et-i      yiy-en adam
            son-his-GEN cat-his meat-ACC eat-PRT man
            "the man whose son's cat ate the meat"

The *en/an* formative might be introduced by a transformation or a base-rule.   If a transformation is used, then
(46) shows that the rule is cyclic or post-cyclic:

(46)   dün        Hasanin    tarafindan öldür-ül-en   çoçuk
       yesterday Hasan-GEN by         kill-PASS-PRT child
       "the child who was killed by Hasan yesterday"

On the reasonable assumption that in Turkish passive sentences the surface subject is derived by promotion of an
underlying object, (46) shows that the marking of the
participle must follow Passive, since it is not until Passive has applied that NP$_{rel}$ is within the subject.   (46)
also shows that if the *en/an* participle is to be introduced
by a base-rule, there will have to be some sort of interpretive principle constraining its distribution that applies
during or after the cycle.

We may further note that the *en/an* participle has the
effect of preventing the subject from taking the genitive
case.   Given a transformational account of *en*-attachment,
we could accommodate this by having *en*-attachment precede
and bleed the nominalization rule.   There would need to be
an additional process to delete NP$_{rel}$.   As in Eskimo, the
nominalization of the verb evidences that S$_{rel}$ is dominated
by an NP node.

I shall now turn to some languages in which pre- and
post relative clauses coexist.

1.1.1.3 *Languages with both Pre- and Post- Relatives:*
Some languages with both types of headed embedded relative

clauses are listed below:

(47)  Classical Tibetan
      Hottentot
      Quechua
      Papago
      Turkish

I shall discuss Turkish, Classical Tibetan and Hottentot.

1.1.1.3.1 *Turkish:* The other Turkish construction consists merely of a clause identical in internal syntax to a
main clause which is introduced by a particle *ki* (derived
from the Persian *ke*). Clauses introduced by *ki* are also
used as subjects and objects of verbs, as are the *ke*-clauses
of Persian. In both the Turkish and Persian relative
clauses with *ki/ke*, the clause is a post-relative and $NP_{rel}$
is deleted. Persian relativization will be discussed later
in this chapter.

Below are some examples of *ki*-clauses in Turkish:

(48)  a.  düşünüyorum ki   Hasan gelecek
          I think        that Hasan will come
          "I think that Hasan will come."

      b.  şüphe-siz     ki  gelecek
          doubt-without that he will come
          "It is without doubt that he will come."

      c.  bir çoçuk ki   kapıyı   kapamaz
          a   child that the door does not close

We note that once again we have a relative clause with
the same form as a nominalization. In this case, of course,
it is fundamentally a fact about Persian, rather than about
Turkish.

Inasmuch as the two relative clause constructions of
Turkish are quite distinct in their internal syntactic con-
structure, I believe that it would be reasonable to derive
them by two distinct base-rules, one generating the pre-
relatives and the other the post-relatives.

1.1.1.3.2 *Classical Tibetan:* This obscure language has
basically SOV word-order. It uses a wide variety of postpositions, and modifiers of nouns can occur on either side
of the head. When modifiers precede the head, they are
followed by a particle whose underlying phonological shape

is *kyi*. Furthermore, the verbs of relative clauses are
nonfinite and take a suffix *pa*, which is of extremely
common use in Tibetan, forming an agent-nominalization,
among other things. Whether *pa* is a relativization marker
or just a general nominalizer I do not know. In a relative
clause, NP$_{rel}$ is somehow deleted.

(49)  a.  bla-ma'i gos
          lama:GEN vestments

          "lama's vestments" (*'i* is a reduced form of *kyi*, and,
          following the conventional usage, I shall label it the
          genitive.  The hyphens in Tibetan transcriptions separ-
          ate syllables, not formatives.)

      b.  skam-pi'i sa
          dry:GEN    earth
          "dry earth"

      c.  čhu   ni bsil-ba-yis
          water    cold   with
          "with cold water"

      d.  saṅs-rgyas-kyi čhös thams-cad yaṅ-dag-par
          Buddha-GEN     law  all        completely
              thob-pa'i      blo
              obtain-REL:GEN intelligence
          "intelligence which completely attains the entire law
          of the Buddha"

      e.  [$_{NP}$ ne-togs daṅ 'bras-bu'i çin-lĵon-pa [$_{S}$ sna-chogs
                  flowers and fruits:GEN trees          $_{rel}$ diverse
              dus    tha-dad-par    dbyuṅ-ba]]
              times  different:LOC bear fruit:REL
          "flowers and fruit trees which at diverse times bear
          different fruit"

(49d) is a relative clause that precedes the head, and (49e)
is one that follows, and we thus find in (49e) no *kyi* following the verb.  Note in (49e) the NP *dus tha-dad-par* 'at
different times', which has the syntactic pattern HEAD-ADJ-
CASE.

These examples show that adjectives and relative clauses
share some of the same syntax in Tibetan. There is still a
question as to what is responsible for the two possible
orders:  either two base orders, as in Turkish, or one base
order and a process of permutation.  It is also worth noting
that *kyi* could not be easily analysed as a Complementizer,
since it appears on adjectives.

1.1.1.3.3 *Hottentot:* In addition to being entertaining in its own right, the evidence from Hottentot provides further argument that embedded relative clauses are constituents with their head, and that they are a category related to adjectives and other nominal modifiers. I shall discuss the Nama dialect.

The basic Hottentot sentence structure is Subject-Verb Phrase. I have not yet untangled the syntax of the verb phrase with its rules for the placement of verb, objects and tense and aspect particles. These rules are quite complex. There is a curious rule which extraposes the subject into the VP and provides it with an accusative case-marker if it is non-initial due to there being an intro-ductory particle or topicalized NP at the front of the S. Furthermore, a clitic copy of the subject is left behind attached to the initial element which triggered movement of the subject. This rule will be seen in action in the relative clause examples.

Hottentot nouns take endings for grammatical gender (masculine, feminine, neuter/common) and number (singular, dual, plural), which are identical with the clitic forms of third person pronouns (the nonclitic forms consist of a stem //*ei* to which appropriate gender endings (i.e. clitic forms) are added). Modifiers, adjectives, possessives, demonstratives and relative clauses may either precede or follow the head. If they follow, the gender-number endings are copied onto them, if they precede, they are not. There is also an accusative case-marker *a* which is attached to the last member of the NP. The language is post-positional, forming possessive phrases with a post-position *di*. These points of Hottentot grammar are illustrated in the following examples:

(50) a. gei /gõa-n
       big  child-N(FUT).PL
       "big children"

     b. //g̃u-b            di  /on-s
        father-M(ASC).SG GEN  name-F(EM).SG
        "the father's name"

c. ao-gu    gei-gu
   man-M.PL big-M.PL
   "the big men"

d. ǂgòa-b  /ằ-s    di-b
   wall-M.SG city-F.SG GEN-M.SG
   "the wall of the city"

e. mũ ta    go  ao-b    gei-b-a
   see I(clitic) PAST man-M.SG big-M.SG-ACC
   "I saw the big men"

Like other modifiers, relative clauses may precede or
follow the head, and when they follow, the agreement marker
of the head shows up on the last word of the clause, which
in all the examples I have found is a verb. When the
clause follows the head, it is introduced by a particle
*hĩa/ia* (I can find no basis for the variation), and when it
precedes, there is no introductory particle. NP$_{rel}$ is
deleted. Note especially that when NP$_{rel}$ is the underlying
subject of S$_{rel}$, there is no clitic form left behind.

(51) a. narí ta gye mũ kho-b    gye ǂgei te
   today I PERF see man-M.SG. PERF call me
   "The man who I saw today called me."

b. khoi-b, ia go //ari    ha-b    gye mĩ
   man-M.SG REL PAST yesterday come-M.SG. PERF say
   "the man who came yesterday said ..."

c. /gõa-b  hĩa-s    tara-s-a    gye si-b    gye
   boy-M.SG. REL-F.SG woman-F.SG.-Acc PERF send-M.SG
   go //hawu
   PAST get lost
   "The boy whom the woman sent got lost."
   (*gye* in the main clause of this example is a sort of
   emphatic particle, not a tense/aspect marker)

d. tara-s    , hia-ts gye sats-a ǂgei ha-s    go
   woman-F.SG   REL-you PERF you-ACC call be-F.SG PAST
   neti ha
   now come
   "the woman whom you called has now come"

Note the subject extraposition, which has applied in
(c-d). Unfortunately, available examples all involve relative clauses modifying the subjects of sentences, so it is
impossible to exhibit the accusative case-marker tacked onto
a relative clause following the head. But the workings of
the agreement rule can be clearly seen. Note that the form

attached to the relative clause is determined by what the head is, and not by what the subject of the clause, is, or any other such thing. These facts show that the Hottentot relative clause is a constituent of an NP containing its head, and has roughly the same external syntax as an adjective.

I shall now turn to some general discussion of the effects of order in the pre- and post- relative clause constructions.

1.1.1.4 *Differences between Pre- and Post- Relatives:* I will here comment on two respects in which the grammar of relative clauses appears to be asymmetrical with respect to linear order. Both observations are quite tentative, and their profferred explanations correspondingly speculative.

First, I believe that pre-relative clauses are more prone than post-relatives to having their subjects put in the genitive case. A functional explanation for this fact is not difficult to think of. In order to avoid center-embedding of S, pre-relative clauses lack COMP or similar introductory particles. The function of a genitive marker on the subject of the relative clause may then be to signal the beginning of a complex constituent: the genitive may serve as a cue that the NP bearing it is not a major constituent of the clause being processed but an initial sub-constituent of a major constituent.

Second, we observed that Japanese lacks any formal distinction of restrictive and nonrestrictive clauses. Such a distinction is also lacking in the other pre-relative clause structures I have examined: Korean, Basque and Turkish.

In Korean[5] we can stack nonrestrictive relations. (52) is a Korean parallel to the Japanese example (40):

(52) $[_{NP}[_{\bar{S}}$ tehak-e     tani-nɪn$][_{NP}[_{\bar{S}}$ ne-ka chowa-ho-n n$][_{NP}$ Mary$]]]$
            college-to go-REL            I NOM like-do-REL     Mary
         "*Mary, who goes to college, who I like"

*nɪn* is a particle that follows relative clauses. This structure is distinct from one in which the two relative clauses are coordinated. I illustrate such a structure in (53):

(53)  [NP[S̄[S[S tehak-e    tani] ko  [S ne-ka chowa-ho]] nɪn]
                college-go go    and     I-NOM like-do    REL
      [NP Mary]]
      "Mary, who goes to college and who I like"

The fact that *nɪn* can be attached to a coordination of S
suggests that it is a *bona fide* occupant of a clause-final
COMP.

Although I know of no language that marks the restric-
tive/nonrestrictive distinction in pre-relative position,
it is not the case that in all languages pre-relatives can
be interpreted nonrestrictively. According to (Perkins
1974), Navajo pre-relatives can only be interpreted res-
trictively, and my own inquiries have confirmed this finding.

We may prevent restrictive and nonrestrictive pre-
relatives from having distinct constituent structures by
requiring in universal grammar that when CP expands to CASE,
NP and S̄, the S̄ follow the NP. There are other aspects to
the distinction in English, such as the requirement that
non-restrictives have a relative pronoun. Their status
is unclear.

With these speculations I end my discussion of pre-
and post- relative clauses.

1.1.2 *Headless Relative Clauses:* There are many languages
in which there are relative clauses which lack a head in
surface structure. Instead, the relative clause appears
dominated by NP, with $NP_{rel}$ being either a pronoun or a
full NP, and perhaps bearing a special mark (such as *wh* in
English).

I propose the following structure (or its mirror-image)
for such relative clauses:

(54)

Most languages appear to have headless relative clauses

in which NP$_{rel}$ is a pronoun. These are generally called
free relative clauses, and have been discussed in English
by Baker (1968) and Kuroda (1969). *Bill ate what was lying
on the table* is a typical free relative clause in English.
Less widespread are those constructions where NP$_{rel}$ is a
full NP. To distinguish these from free relatives I shall
follow Gorbet (1974) in calling them internal head relatives. Such a relative clause in English is *what beer we
drank was flat*. In English, the internal head relative
clause is a very minor construction, but in other languages,
such as Diegueño and Navajo, it is the major vehicle of
relativization.

Internal head relative clauses may coexist in a language with either pre- or post- relative clauses, and in some
languages, such as Diegueño, may be the only kind of relative clause other than free relatives. In this language,
internal head relative clauses coexist with a variety of
structures whose analysis is dubious.

Below I give a list of languages having internal head
relative clauses, indicating whether they coexist with pre-
or post- relative clauses:

(55) Languages with Internal Head Relative Clauses:

| Hopi | (pre-) | Crow | (pre-) |
|------|--------|------|--------|
| Navajo | (post-) | Diegueno | (pre- and post- ?) |
| Dagbani | (pre-) | English | (pre-) |

In this section I will discuss Navajo and English. Later
in the chapter I will consider Dagbani and Crow. Diegueno
receives a major treatment in (Gorbet 1974), and Hopi is
discussed in (Jeanne 1974).

1.1.2.1 *Navajo:* Navajo is an SOV language with postpositions and conjunctions that follow the subordinate
clauses they are associated with.

I shall identify four relative clause constructions in
Navajo: a free relative, indistinguishable in form from a
kind of indirect question, a pre-relative, an internal head
relative, and an extraposed relative. My information on
these constructions is drawn from (Platero 1974), (Kaufman
1974) and (Perkins 1975). The latter types appear to be

related to each other as against the free relatives.
Therefore, after some more general discussion of Navajo
grammar, I will first discuss the pre-, internal head and
extraposed relatives, and then turn to the free relatives.
My discussion on many points will be incomplete, as a much
fuller treatment is given in (Platero 1974) and (Kaufman
1974).

Navajo has agreement processes whereby verbs are marked
for the person and number of their subjects and objects.
Postpositions are also marked for these features of their
objects, and possessed NP for these features of their
possessors. In the examples here we shall see only marking
of verbs. The agreement markers are prefixes, and are
placed in the order *Object-prefix Subject-Prefix*, and are
interspersed with a great variety of other prefixes of
diverse functions. We shall encounter a future tense, and
perfective and imperfective aspects (IMP and PERF). Phonological rules of great complexity obscure the underlying
form and arrangement of the prefixes, rendering futile any
attempt to gloss formatives in the surface phonological
form. The phonology is discussed in (Stanley 1969).

We thus have the simple transitive and intransitive
sentences (56):

(56)  a.  ashkii ałháá'
          boy    IMP:3:snore
          "the boy is snoring"

      b.  ashkii at'ééd yiztał
          boy    girl   3:PERF:3:kick
          "the boy kicked the girl"

There is an interesting rule of Subject-object inversion, which interchanges the positions of subject and
object, and replaces *yi*, the 3rd person object prefix for
transitive verbs, with *bi*. Applying this rule to (56b) we
get (57):

(57)  at'ééd ashkii biztał
      girl   boy    3:PERF:kick
      "the girl was kicked by the boy"

All relative clauses end in a formative *í(gíí)* or its
alternate *ęę* (sometimes *ąą* due to phonology), which is a

complementizer used in various sorts of nominal subordinate clauses other than relative clauses. These complementizers are discussed extensively in (Kaufman 1974). $NP_{rel}$ in a relative clause can be subject, object, possessor, or the object of a postposition. I will illustrate the first two possibilities. The others may be found in (Platero 1974).

(58) is an intransitive clause. In (59 a, b, c) I embed it as a pre-, internal head and extraposed relative, respectively:

(58)  tl'éédą́ą́'  ashkii ałháá'
      last:night boy    IMP:3:snore
      "the boy was snoring last night"

(59) a.  tl'éédą́ą́  ałháá'-ą́ą      ashkii yádoołtih
         last:night IMP:3:snore-REL boy    FUT:3:speak

     b.  tl'éédą́ą́  ashkii ałháá'-ą́ą      yádoołtih
         last:night boy    IMP:3:snore-REL FUT:3:speak

     c.  ashkii yádoołtih    tl'éédą́ą́  ałháá'-ą́ą
         boy    FUT:3:speak last:night 3:PAST:snore-REL

         "the boy who was snoring last night will speak"

The clause internal position of *ashkii* in (59b) shows that it is $NP_{rel}$ rather than $NP_{hd}$.

(60) is a transitive clause with first person subject, and in (61) I embed it in the three constructions just as in (59):

(60)  łééchąą'í sétał
      dog       3:PERF:1:kick
      "I kicked the dog"

(61) a.  sétał-éé          łééchąą'í nahał'in
         3:PERF:1:kick-REL dog       IMP:3:bark

     b.  łééchąą'í sétał-éé          nahał'in
         dog       3:PERF:1:kick-REL IMP:3:bark

         łééchąą'í nahał'in    sétał-éé
         dog       IMP:3:bark 3:PERF:1:kick-REL

         "the dog that I kicked is barking"

A question that arises immediately, especially in the light of some of the constructions we will be considering in section 1.1.3., is how we know that the purported internal head relative clauses of (59b) and (61c) are actually

dominated by NP, taking the place of ordinary nouns in the
syntactic structure of their matrices. We can see this by
observing examples in which there are internal head relative clauses both in object and in subject position, and in
which the subject-object inversion rule applies:

(62)  a.  adą́ą́dą́ą́'  shi-zhé'é  łį́į́  nayiisnii'-ę́ę
          yesterday my-father horse 3:PERF:3:buy-REL

          ashkii łééchąą'i bishxash-ę́ę        yiztał
          boy    dog        3:PERF:3:buy-REL 3:PERF:3:kick

       "the horse which my father bought yesterday kicked the
       dog which bit the boy" or
       "the horse which my father bought yesterday kicked the
       boy whom the dog bit"

      b.  ashkii łééchąą'i bishxash-ę́ę        adą́ą́dą́ą́'  shi-zhé'é
          boy    dog        3:PERF:3:bite-REL yesterday my-father

          łį́į́'  nayiisnii'-ę́ę       biztał
          horse 3:PERF:3:buy-REL 3:PERF:3:kick

       (same as (62a) in meaning)

We see that the internal head construction is subject
to considerable ambiguity: *ashkii łééchąą'i bishxashę́ę* in
(62) can be interpreted either as "the boy who the dog bit"
or "the dog that bit the boy" (note the application of
Subject-object inversion in the relative clause).

We would expect the pre-relative construction to likewise be ambiguous. But in that structure, there are principles discussed by Platero that eliminate ambiguity in
most cases. (63a) thus gets the reading (63b) but not
(63c):

(63)  a.  ashkii yiyiiłtsá-(n)ę́ę at'ééd yáłtih
          boy    3:PERF:see-REL girl   IMP:3:speak

      b.  the girl who saw the boy is speaking

      c.  *the girl who the boy saw is speaking

Platero proposes to derive the three structures we have
been considering from a common source: a prerelative
structure in which $NP_{rel}$ and $NP_{hd}$ are represented by full
NP. The extraposed relatives are derived by a rule of
extraposition. Evidence against this discovered by Perkins
(1975) will be discussed in section 1.1.3.6. Here I shall
discuss and criticize the proposed derivation of pre- and

internal head relatives.

By Platero's proposal, the common source for the examples of (61) will be (64):

(64)

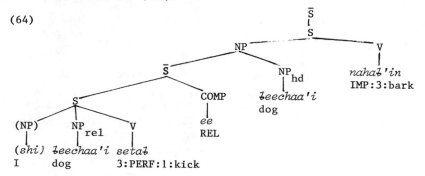

We can apply deletion forwards, deleting $NP_{hd}$ and deriving (61b), or we can apply deletion backwards, deleting $NP_{rel}$ to derive (61a). There are thus no internal head relative clauses in underlying structure.

Platero hypothesizes that the deletion rule applying in relative clauses is the same as ordinary pronominalization, which in Navajo may be effected by deletion. Pronominalization by deletion may go forwards, or backwards into a subordinate clause. These points are illustrated in example (65), in which there is an initial subordinate clause in the adverbial complementizer go:

(65) a. ashkii yah-iiya-(a)go   neezdá
        boy    into-PERF:3:go-COMP PERF:3:sit

     b. yah-'iiya-(a)go      ashkii neezdá
        into-PERF:3:go-COMP boy    PERF:3:sit
        "when the boy$_i$ came in, he$_i$ sat down"

Between coordinated clauses we can delete forwards, but not backwards:

(66) a. ashkii yah-'iiyá      dóó neezdá
        boy    into-PERF:3:go and PERF:3:sit
        "the boy entered and sat down"

     b. yah-'iiya        doo ashkii neezda
        into-PERF:3:go and boy    PERF:3:sit
        "he$_i$ entered and the boy$_j$ sat down"

This restriction manifests itself in the relative clause system as the fact that in the extraposed construction

$NP_{hd}$ cannot be deleted:

(67) *nahał'in    łééchąą'í sétał-ęę
IMP:3:bark dog        3:PERF:1:kick
"the dog that I kicked was barking"

Platero observes a significant defect of this solution, which is that while the deletion effected by ordinary pro- nominalization is optional, in the relative clause con- struction either $NP_{rel}$ or $NP_{hd}$ must go. Hence we have (68) as an alternative to (65), and (69) as an alternative to (66):

(68) ashkii yah-'ííyá-(a)go    ashkii neezdá
boy    into-PERF:3:go-COMP boy    PERF:3:sit
"when the boy$_i$ came in, the boy$_i$ sat down"

(69) ashkii yah-'ííyá-(a)go    dóó ashkii neezdá
boy    into-PERF:3:go-COMP and boy    PERF:3:sit
"the boy$_i$ entered and the boy$_i$ sat down"

But (70), the sentence derived from (64) by applying no transformations, is ungrammatical:

(70) *łééchąą'í sétał-ęę        łééchąą'í nahał'in
dog    3:PERF:1:kick-REL dog        IMP:3:bark
"the dog I kicked is barking"

In his article, Platero suggested that perhaps deletion of $NP_{rel}$ was optional in extraposed relative clauses, but he stated that this was not true for all speakers, and has since then decided (personal communication) that deletion of $NP_{rel}$ is obligatory in these structures.

Platero and Hale (1974) propose a reanalysis in which an internal head structure is underlying for the relative clause, and the head is extracted optionally. A further alternative would be to say that there are underlyingly both pre- and internal head relative structures, and that deletion of $NP_{rel}$ is obligatory in the pre-relative. On either of these analyses, the obligatory disappearance of $NP_{rel}$ in the pre-relative construction is easily accounted for.

These analyses are also rendered more attractive by the fact that, as we shall shortly see, internal head relative clauses may co-exist with post-relatives as well as pre-relatives. A rule deleting the head of a post-relative clause on identity to $NP_{rel}$ would violate the normal conditions on deletion. Other arguments against head-deletion will also be adduced.

I finally observe that the relative clause constructions in Navajo cannot be used nonrestrictively. Hence the following are all ungrammatical:

> (71) a. *Kii sétaɬ-ę́ę neezdá
> Kii 3:PERF:1:kick-REL PERF:3:sit
> "Kii, who I kicked, sat down"
>
> b. *sétaɬ-ę́ę Kii neezdá
> 3:PERF:1:kick-REL Kii PERF:3:sit
> "Kii, who I kicked, sat down"
>
> c. *Kii neezdá sétaɬ-ę́ę
> Kii PERF:3:sit 3:PERF:1:kick-REL
> "Kii sat down, who I kicked"

One might be tempted to associate the absence of a nonrestrictive interpretation with the hypothesis that underlying internal head structures cannot be interpreted nonrestrictively: this would entail accepting a head-extraction analysis for the pre-relative structures. This suggestion is obviously highly speculative.

I shall now briefly consider the free relative clauses. I shall consider them only in connection with another construction, the enclitic phrase. The enclitics are a class of particles that are suffixed to NP and PP in order to express various notions of direction and other concepts associated with motion and location. With the enclitic *di* "at," we can thus form (72):

> (72) hastiin kin-di sidá
> man house-at IMP:3:sit
> "the man is sitting at the house"

Platero (1974) notes two presumably related peculiarities of enclitics: their object NP cannot take demonstratives, and their object NP cannot be relativized:

> (73) a. *shí díí tsékooh-di sédá
> I this canyon-at IMP:1:sit
> "I am sitting in this canyon"

b.  *hastiin kin-di    sidá-(h)ígíí naa'íízhoozh
    man     house-in IMP:3:sit-REL PERF:3:collapse
    "the house the man was sitting in collapsed"

With free relatives, however, we find the situation quite
different.

Kaufman (1974) observes a construction that appears
to be used both as an indirect question and as a free relative clause.  The target NP of the construction can be an
enclitic phrase with no full NP head, and the enclitic
migrates to the *í(gíí)/ę́ę̨* COMP that terminates both constructions.

(74) illustrates the construction used as an indirect
question:

(74) díí bilagáanaa diné   bizaad  yíhool'áá'aa-di
     this whiteman  Navajo language 3:PERF:3:learn:COMP-at
         doo shił   béehózin-da
         NEG 1:with 3:know-NEG
     "I don't know where this Anglo learned Navajo."

The use as a free relative is illustrated by (75):

(75) gałbáhí a'áán-góne' yah-eelwod-í-gí     hatl'éé'
     rabbit  hole-in    into-PERF:3:run-REL-at area is dark
     "It is dark in the area around where the rabbit ran into
        the hole"
    *"It's dark in the hole which the rabbit ran into"

The second, incorrect, translation is what the sentence
would mean if it were a relative clause on *a'aangóne'*
'in the hole.'  Instead, it appears to be a free relative
on a deleted enclitic phrase with the enclitic *gi* 'at,' the
free relative giving the location around where the rabbit
ran into the hole.

Any number of things might be happening with these
constructions. They might be superficially homophonous but
underlyingly distinct constructions, as are the free relatives and indirect questions of English.  On the other hand,
they might all syntactically be free relatives, with the
'indirect question' of (74) a kind of 'concealed question'
(see Baker 1968).  What seems certain, however, is that
free relatives have some significantly different properties
from the others.

Here I conclude my discussion of Navajo.

**1.1.2.2** *English*: We observed above that in addition to free relatives and *ever*-clauses, English has an internal head relative clause exemplified in such examples as *what beer we found was flat*. I shall first distinguish this latter construction, which for reasons that will become apparent I will call the paucal relative, from the others, and then I will provide an argument that in paucal and in free relatives the *wh*-marked NP is a constituent of the relative clause rather than a head. Finally, I will briefly consider a reason to suspect that the *wh*-marked NP may be generated in initial position rather than preposed.

The paucal relative looks like a free relative with a full head nominal supplied. Perhaps the first thing we notice is that we can only supply such a nominal when the NP is plural or mass:

(76)  a.  I drank what was provided.
     b.  I drank what beer was provided.
     c.  *I drank what glass of milk was provided.

(77)  a.  Fred hit what was on the table
     b.  Fred hit what weapons were on the table.
     c.  *Fred hit what weapon was on the table.

This requirement that the NP be non-individual (see Fiengo 1974) distinguishes the paucal relative not only from the free relative, but also from the *whatever*-clause, insasmuch as we can say *Fred hid whatever weapon was on the table*.

We may next observe that while we can add the paucal quantifiers *few* and *little* to NP$_{rel}$ in the paucal construction, these are the only quantifiers that may be added:

(78)  a.  Fred hid what few weapons were on the table.
     b.  Bill drank what little wine we had.
     c.  *I saw what three people arrived early.
     d.  *I know what many people came to the party.

With the *whatever* construction, numerals, but not paucal quantifiers are possible:

(79)  a.  *I greeted whatever few people came to the door.
     b.  I hid the coats of whatever three people he brought.

(79b) is not terribly good, and for many other quantifiers the judgements are too shady for me to wish to make any claims about them.

We may finally observe that the paucal relative clause makes the imputation that the referent of the clause is present in meagre, insufficient amounts. Hence (79b) implies that not much beer was provided, and (77b) that not many weapons were on the table. Nonetheless, this imputation seems to be weaker than it would be were a paucal quantifier present, as may be seen by examining (78a, b); and examples can be found where the imputation of paucity is very weak or perhaps nonexistent: *we will take what steps are necessary*.

Nonetheless as a preliminary explanation I shall propose that there is an underlying element PAUC in the quantifier phrase position of the paucal relatives without overt surface quantifier. PAUC is an abstract member of the class otherwise comprising *few* and *little*, and it is weaker in force. By supposing that it shares with *few* and *little* the requirement that the quantified NP be non-individual, we may explain the impossibility of count singular heads in the paucal construction, as well as the interpretation of the clauses.

While the postulation of abstract elements in syntax is dangerous, it is worth pointing out that the quantifiers are a closed rather than an open class, so that their members may be distinguished from each other by a finite set of features that may be properly said to be a part of the grammar of the language. We can thus treat PAUC as the archi-quantifier embracing *few* and *little*. The effect of our analysis is to connect the requirement that the relative NP be non-individual with the restrictions on the quantifiers possible for this NP.

We now turn to the problem of proving that the *wh*-NP in the free and paucal relative constructions are really constituents of the relative clause. I shall first offer and dispose of a potential argument that does not go through, and then establish the point by a consideration of the behaviour of returning pronouns.

50

We may observe that the free and paucal relatives do
not permit the *wh* NP to be followed by the particle that:

(80)  a.  *I drank what (little) beer that was on the table.

     b.  *I drank what (little) beer that we found.

     c.  *I ate what that we brought.

It strikes me that the *that* is much better with the paucals
(80a, b) than with the free relative (80c). I have no
explanation for this.

This argument fails to fully convince, because Ø, *that*
and relative pronouns are not in free variation as initials
for relative clauses in English. Consider the following
series of examples:

(81)  a.  I met a girl I liked.

     b.  I met a girl that I liked.

     c.  I met a girl who I liked.

(81a) has the sense that I met one of the girls who I liked,
while (81c) means most preferably that I met a girl and
liked her. (81b) appears to be ambiguous. (I am indebted
to William Cantrall for some discussion of these and related subtleties of meaning). The 'contact' relative construction, the one with neither *that* nor relative pronouns,
thus appears to be distinct from the other two, as they are
from each other. We could therefore claim that the free
and paucal relatives consisted of a *wh* marked NP as head
together with a contact relative.

We now consider the argument from the behaviour of
returning pronouns. Returning pronouns are pronouns occupying the pre-*wh* movement or relative pronoun deletion
position of $NP_{rel}$. They are fully grammatical in certain
geographical regions, such as Texas, and many other speakers,
such as myself, are highly tolerant of them. In the following examples we see returning pronouns:

(82)  a.  The people who Bill says that they stole
        his car are standing over there.

     b.  He is a criminal that the FBI will be pleased
        if they catch him.

Carlson and Martin (1974) note a restriction that resumptive

pronouns must be fairly deeply embedded in the relative
clause in order to be acceptable, and that they sound best
if they are in a position from which island constraints and
other such restrictions would prevent one from moving or
deleting a pronoun. Hence *the girl who I saw her* is
ungrammatical.

I will here note two further restrictions on returning
pronouns. First observe that they can occur neither with
questions nor with free relatives:

(83)  a.  the ice-cream that Fred says if you eat it you'll
          get off has been withdrawn from the market

      b.  the automobile that the policeman who impounded
          it got a citation was a Buick

(84)  a.  *what does Fred think (that) if you eat it you'll
          get off?

      b.  *what (automobile) did the policeman who impounded
          it get a citation?

(85)  a.  *what Fred says (that) if you eat it you'll get off
          has been withdrawn from the market

      b.  *what the policeman who impounded it got a citation
          is being held at the courthouse

(86)  a.  *what few drugs Fred says (that) if you take them
          you'll get off have been withdrawn from the market

      b.  *what few weapons the policemen who impounded them
          got citations are being held at the courthouse.

We may next observe that even in a headed relative clause
returning pronouns cannot co-refer with a constituent preposed by pied piping:

(87)  a.  *There is the boy whose mother Bill says that
          she's a stripper.

      b.  *This is the car the owner of which the patrolman
          who arrested him got a citation.

We can see from (83-87) the generalisation that a returning
pronoun is ungrammatical without a head with which it can
corefer without anomaly. In (84-86) there is no head at
all, and in (87) the returning pronoun cannot be coreferential with the head without destroying the semantic interpretation of the clause. It is clear that if the *wh*-NP

of (85-86) were analysed $NP_{hd}$ rather than as $NP_{rel}$ we could
not achieve this unification of restrictions on returning
pronouns.

I shall finally observe a reason for suspecting that
the $NP_{rel}$ in the headless relative constructions are generated in COMP position. It was observed by Joan Bresnan (in
as yet unpublished work) that pied piping is impossible with
free relatives.  It is also impossible with paucal relatives:

(88)  a.  I stole what Bill was writing with.

      b.  *I stole with what Bill was writing.

(89)  a.  Bill alienated what few girls he danced with.

      b.  *Bill alienated with what few girls he danced.

We might semantically analyse a relative clause as consisting of a sentence open on a variable $x$ to which an
operator R binding $x$ is prefixed.  We might further suppose
that the operator is restricted by whatever nominal material
is in $NP_{rel}$.  Hence *who Bill saw* would translate as
(R $x$:human) (Bill saw $x$).  R would be interpreted in the
obvious way as an abstraction operator.  Now suppose that a
*wh*-NP that is in an ordinary sentence-internal position is
preposed in the translation from syntactic to semantic
structure, but that one that is in COMP position is merely
left in place, with the S translating into a sentence open
on some position which in the syntax is 'empty.'  Then *what
few people I saw* will translate out as (R $x$:few people)
(I saw $x$), but *with what few people he danced* will come out
as (with (R $x$:with few people)) (he danced?) or some similar
piece of garbage, provided that the *wh*-phrases are underlyingly initial.  I suggest, then, that it might be the
case that (a) semantic interpretation precedes *wh*-movement
and works in the manner suggested (b) headed relatives and
questions don't (or needn't) have their *wh* NP in COMP position (c) headless relatives require their *wh* NP to be in
initial position.  This must, of course, all be regarded as
the rankest speculation.

I will close with the observation that the free and
paucal relative clauses would both correspond to restrictive

relative clause with definite heads when rendered in a
headed construction.  Likewise, the Navajo relative clause,
which Hale and Platero (1974) suspect to have an underlyingly headless structure (pre-relatives being derived by extraction), also corresponds only to a restrictive relative
on a definite head.  Such interpretations may then be a
universal property of the headless relative, and there may
thereby be a way to distinguish pre- and post-relatives
that are derived by extraction from those that are not.
This too must be regarded as highly speculative.

1.1.3 *Adjoined Relative Clauses:*  Adjoined relative clauses
appear not within an NP in their matrix S, but rather at
the beginning or the end of that S, possibly separated from
their head by an unbounded stretch of material.

I propose that adjoined relative clauses come in three
varieties:  anticipatory, extraposed and trailing.  Anticipatory and trailing relatives I propose to be generated by
a rule $\bar{S} \longrightarrow$ COMP $(\bar{S})$ S $(\bar{S})$, the first $\bar{S}$ on the right being
anticipatory, the second being trailing.  Extraposed rela-
tives I propose to be introduced by S $\longrightarrow$ S $\bar{S}$.  Extraposed
relatives are the extraposed relatives familiar from Eng-
lish, while anticipatory and trailing relatives are a type
that is present in English only in the form of an assortment of marginal constructions, but is in many languages
the major vehicle of relativization. The justifications for
distinguishing trailing from extraposed relatives will
emerge gradually:  essentially the trailing relative is a
counterpart to the anticipatory relative, while the extraposed relative is related to the embedded relative.  It is
obvious that these structural proposals are tremendously
oversimplified.  There is need for a great deal more work
on the ways in which subordinate clauses may be attached to
the margins of matrices.  Nonetheless the present proposal
will suffice as a beginning.

We thus attain the following three constituent structures for relative clauses not forming a constituent with
their head:

54

(90)　a.　Anticipatory Relative:

b.　Trailing Relative:

c.　Extraposed Relative:

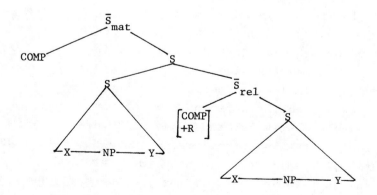

Some languages with anticipatory and trailing relative clauses as major relative clause structures are the following:

(91)  Languages with Anticipatory and Trailing Relatives:

| Warlpiri |  | Sanskrit |
|----------|--|----------|
| Mabuiag | Australian | Bengali |
| Kaititj |  | Hindi |
| Papago |  | Marathi |
| Hittite |  | Bambara |

English and Navajo have extraposed relatives without anticipatory relatives (excepting marginal constructions in
English).

I shall first discuss the Australian languages Warlpiri
and Mabuiag, then the Indic languages Hindi, Sanskrit and
Marathi, and finally, Navajo and English.  Among the high-
lights will be the exhibition of double headed anticipatory relatives in Sanskrit and Marathi, double headed
extraposed relatives in English and Navajo, and finally,
cases from Marathi and Navajo where adjoined relatives are
separated from their heads by unbounded stretches of material.  Such cases have also been given for Hindi by Satyanarayana and Subbarao (1973).

1.1.3.1.  *Warlpiri*:  This is a somewhat oversimplified
account of material presented by Ken Hale in class (1971).[7]
I am of course responsible for any errors in the presen-
tation.

Warlpiri is a basically SOV language with very free
scrambling and a case system including ergative, absolutive,
dative, etc.  A constituent with considerable presence in
the surface structure is an Aux-node, the contents of which
are realized as a single word and which contains tense/
aspect and mood markers, as well as agreement morphemes
expressing the case and number of various complements of
the verb.  Curiously, the case-system of the agreement
formatives is nominative-accusative while that of the NP is
ergative-absolutive.  This suggests that the underlying
case system is nominative-accusative, and that after the
agreement rule applies, an ergative-absolutive rule applies
to the full NP and causes the earlier nominative-accusative
marking to be obliterated.

Warlpiri speakers do not like constituents of more than
one word length to appear in surface structure, preferring

to scramble apart even such constituents as NP consisting
of head and adjective or demonstrative. Especially, Warlpiri speakers do not like embedded S, and sentences with
center-embedded S are definitely ungrammatical in Warlpiri.
Thus there are both anticipatory and trailing relative
clauses, but no embedded relatives.

In a relative clause, there is a formative *kutja* at the
beginning of the AUX, to which various tense-aspect and
agreement markers (which may add up to $\emptyset$, since many of
them are $\emptyset$) are added. In the simplest constructions,
whichever of $NP_{rel}$ or $NP_{hd}$ comes second may be deleted, or
both may be left untouched. It is hence reasonable to
believe that in this language, the deletions are accomplished by pronominalization, as is not the case in Navajo.

Below are some examples:

(92) a. timana-ḷu $\emptyset$  kuḍu  kutju-ṇu
horse-ERG AUX child throw-PAST
"the horse threw the child."

b. ŋatju ka-ṇa-ḷa      kuḍu-ku   maritjari-mi
I     PRES-1-3(DAT) child-DAT feel sorry for-NONPAST
"I feel sorry for the child."

c. ṭimana-ḷu kutja kuḍu  kutju-ṇu  ŋatju ka-ṇa-ḷa
horse-ERG REL   child throw-PAST I     PRES-1-3(DAT)
(kuḍu-ku)  maritjari-mi
child-DAT) feel sorry for-NONPAST
"I feel sorry for the child that the horse threw."

d. ŋatju ka-ṇa-ḷa      kuḍu-ku   maritjari-mi
I     PRES-1-3(DAT) child-DAT feel sorry for-NONPAST
ṭimana-ḷu kutja kutju-ṇu  (kuḍu)
horse-ERG REL   throw-PAST (child)
"I feel sorry for the child that the horse threw."

The surface independence of the relative clause from its
head is shown by the fact that there is no necessary constituent structure relationship holding between $NP_{hd}$ and $S_{rel}$,
and by the fact that the case-marking of $NP_{hd}$ and $NP_{rel}$ is
entirely determined by the role each NP plays in its clause.

Sometimes, when under great stress, Warlpiri speakers
violate the rule against embedding relative clauses, and
then a relative gets stuffed into an NP between the head
and the case-marker. In this construction, the clauses
look like an adjective formating a surface constituent

with its head. I believe that such relative clauses are
ungrammatical, because Hale reports that a Warlpiri speaker
will not admit that he pronounced such a sentence, even if
confronted with tape-recorded evidence, much less admit
that they are possible in Warlpiri.

From this ungrammatical embedded structure, one can
actually get up an argument against deriving relative
clauses from an embedded source:  for when an ordinary
adjective is removed from an NP it takes along with it a
copy of the case-marker of the NP.  Therefore, if relative
clause were to move out of an NP, one would expect it to
take with it the case-marker of that NP.

A construction like that of Warlpiri obviously puts
strong limitations on the number of relative clauses that
can occur modifying NP in a single S.  The structure I have
given permits two, but it is difficult to tell whether two
or one is the permitted number.  Only one relative clause
can occur at either end of the S, but the occurrence of S
with relative clauses at both ends as made possible by my
$\bar{S} \rightarrow$ COMP $(\bar{S})$ S $(\bar{S})$ rule is doubtful.  Hale reports that
when such structures occur, the following relative clause
has very much the flavour of an after-thought.  A construction that suggests that the trailing relative clause in
such cases is an afterthought is an extremely common one
in which the trailing relative clause is a copy of the
anticipatory one, giving such a sentence as *the man came
yesterday, I hit the man, the man came yesterday* as a
rendition of *I hit the man who came yesterday*.  Perhaps the
second relative clause is tacked on because the speaker has
forgotten about the first.  The 'afterthoughtty' character
of many trailing relative clauses is interesting in light
of the fact that Thiersch (1974) has observed similar properties of clauses in English that I will in section
1.1.3.7  analyse as trailing clauses.

I have already noted that whichever of $NP_{rel}$ and $NP_{hd}$
comes second is optionally deletable, and since Warlpiri
has widespread deletion of anaphoric pronouns, we can
safely assume that this optional deletion is accomplished

by pronominalization. There are other more complicated configurations involving determiners in which $NP_{rel}$ and $NP_{hd}$ may appear, but since I have not determined their relation to other sorts of anaphoric processes, I shall not discuss them here.

Warlpiri supports the $\bar{\bar{S}} \to COMP\ (\bar{S})\ S\ (\bar{S})$ rule, inasmuch as (a) there is no evidence that relative clauses are extracted from their heads, and (b) if relative clauses were extracted from their heads, there would be no way to capture the one-to-a-side restriction.

1.1.3.2 *Mabuiag*: I will here briefly sketch some of the results arrived at by T. Klokeid (1970) in his research on Mabuiag, another Australian language. Klokeid identifies three types of relative clauses: participials, which appear to be some sort of reduced relative, and are hence beyond the scope of this paper; full relatives with a *wh* word; and full relatives without such a word. The former type occurs in both anticipatory and trailing position, the latter only in trailing position.

I will first discuss the clauses without a *wh*-word. These clauses are always anticipatory, and $NP_{rel}$ remains a full NP within them, exactly as it would in an unembedded S. $NP_{hd}$, which always follows the relative clause, may either be deleted or pronominalized. Deletion is a regular alternative to pronominalization. One suspects that $NP_{hd}$ could also be left intact, but Klokeid does not give us information on this point.

Some examples are:

(93)  a.  moegekaz$_i$ uzarai-dhin Panai-ka, Zon $\begin{Bmatrix} \emptyset_i \\ \text{nubi -ka}_i \end{Bmatrix}$
          child$_i$  go-PAST      Panai-DAT John him-DAT$_i$
          mulai-dhin
          talk-PAST
          "John talked to the child who went to Panai."

      b.  moegekazi-n$_i$ gulaig$_j$ gasam-dhin, $\begin{Bmatrix} \emptyset \\ \text{nui} \end{Bmatrix}$ $\begin{matrix} i \text{ or } j \\ i \text{ or } j \end{matrix}$
          child-ERG$_i$   captain touch-PAST  he$_i$
          uzarai-dhin Panai-ka
          go-PAST      Panai-DAT
          "The child who touched the captain went to Panai."
          "The captain who the child touched went to Panai."

The same essential considerations apply here as do in Warlpiri: there is no compelling reason for deriving these clauses from anywhere but from where they appear in surface structure.

These relative clauses are identical in form to a sort of *because*-clause. In the *because*-clause, there needn't be any NP coreferential with anything in the main clause, but if there is, it gets pronominalized or deleted, just as when a relative clause is present. Hence the examples of (93) also have the *because*-clause readings "John talked to the captain because he went to Panai" and "the captain went to Panai because the child touched him" or "the child went to Panai because he touched the captain". Therefore, if the base rules which generated the *because*-clauses also generated the anticipatory relative clauses, no great syntactic implausibilities would result.

The other form of relative clause uses a *'wh'* word *ngadh* (occurring, of course, in many case-forms) as a relative pronoun or relative determiner of NP. One would of course presume that the uses as pronoun and determiner are in fact the same, the pronominal use being when pronominalization has removed the rest of the NP. *ngadh* is also used as the interrogative pronoun-determiner, as well as as an identity-of-sense pronoun like English *one* in *a red one*. Clauses with *ngadh* can never be interpreted as *because*-clauses, and they may either precede or follow the matrix. They may also occur as post-relatives, but this construction is strained, and is said to have weird intonation.

Some examples of relative clauses with *ngadh* are the following:

(94) a. ngadh mabaig-an os  guudthapam-dhin uzarai-dhin
       Wh-ERG man-ERG  horse kiss-PAST      go-PAST
         Bessai-da
         Bessai-DAT
       "The man who kissed a horse went to Bessai".

     b. mabaig uzarai-dhin Bessai-ka, ngadh  mabaig-an os
        man    go-PAST     Bessai-DAT wh-ERG man-ERG    horse
          guudthapam-dhin
          kiss-PAST
        "The man who kissed a horse went to Bessai".

```
(c)   Zon  mabaig, ngadh  os      guudthapam-dhin, matham-dhin
      John man      wh-ERG horse kiss-PAST         hit-PAST
      "John hit the man who kissed the horse."
```

The greater positional freedom of the clause with *ngadh*
is probably a consequence of the fact that it contains a
signal that it is a subordinate clause:  if the relative
clause without *ngadh* were permitted to occur both at the
beginning and the end of the main clause, it would be
impossible to tell which was which.  I am not sure how such
a constraint should be built into the grammar.

Mabauiag is like Warlpiri in having relative clauses
introduced by the $\bar{S} \longrightarrow$ COMP $(\bar{S})$ S $(\bar{S})$ rule, and in having
pronominalization processes be the ones responsible for
reducing whichever of $NP_{hd}$ and $NP_{rel}$ gets reduced;  but
unlike Warlpiri, it optionally has a special determiner for
$NP_{rel}$, and there is a slight possibility for there to be
post-relative clauses of some sort as well.  We shall see
that on the whole, the relative clauses introduced by
$\bar{S} \longrightarrow$ COMP $(\bar{S})$ S $(\bar{S})$ do not have special rules deleting
$NP_{rel}$.

1.1.3.3  *Hindi*:  In this subsection, I will briefly summarize the main points of relativization in Hindi as described
by Donaldson (1971).  Relative clauses may be anticipatory,
trailing, or embedded as post-relatives.  $NP_{rel}$ has a relative determiner *jo* (occurring in many inflectional forms)
which is distinct from the interrogative pronoun.  $NP_{hd}$ has
the demonstrative determiner *vǝh* (also occurring in many
inflectional forms) which normally means 'that'.  As in the
preceding languages, whichever of $NP_{rel}$ and $NP_{hd}$ comes
second has everything but the determiner optionally deleted,
presumably by pronominalization.  Hence Hindi is essentially
similar to Mabuiag.  Hindi provides the pattern for the
other Indic languages:  hence, I will discuss in later
sections examples from Sanskrit and Marathi without going
into great detail with these languages.

Below are a series of examples from Hindi, first preposed relatives (95), then extraposed (96), and finally
post-relatives (97):

(95) a. Jo ləṛka mere pas rəhta hai, vəh mera choṭa bhaii hai.
wh boy me near lives that my little brother is
"The boy who lives near me is my little brother."

b. Mere pas jo ləṛka rəhta hai, vəh mera choṭa bhaii
me near wh boy lives that my little brother
hai.
is
"The boy who lives next door to me is my little brother."

c. Jo per nadii ke kinare pər tha, pəkshii us pər
wh tree river of bank on was bird that on
baiṭha tha.
sitting was
"The bird was sitting on the tree that was on the bank
of the river."

(95b) reveals that the *wh*-word needn't front, while (95c)
shows $S_{rel}$ and $NP_{hd}$ separated by the subject of the matrix
S, so that they cannot be a constituent.

(96) a. Vəh ləṛka mera choṭa bhaii hai, jo mere pas rəhta
that boy my little brother is wh me near
hai.
lives
"The boy who lives near me is my little brother."

b. Gay sərək cəlii ja rəhii thii, log jis pər baiṭhe
cow street on going was people wh on sitting
hue the.
were
"The cow was walking on the street on which people were
sitting." (I don't understand why there is no *vəh*
with *sərək*)

(97) a. Ram ne, jo əmiir hai, ek məkan khəriida
Ram INSTR wh rich is a house bought
"Ram, who is rich, bought a house."

b. Us admii ne, jo əmiir hai, ek məkan khəriida.
that man INSTR wh rich is a house bought
"The man who is rich bought a house."

The instrumental cases on the subject NP in the matrices of
(97) are due to the fact that in certain tenses, the subject
is put in the instrumental.

There are various special points to be made. First,
when the head noun is definite, as we have seen, it usually
acquires the determiner *vəh* 'that.' Ordinary definite NP
bear no determiner at all. But if the head NP bears the
determiner *yəh* 'this', it keeps this determiner, as shown
in (98) below:

(98)  Yəh  kal  shant      nəhĩĩ  hai  jisme  həm  rəhte  hai.
      this  age  peaceful  not   is   wh-in  we   live
      "This age in which we live is not peaceful."

Secondly, there is a restriction that if the head NP is indefinite, with the determiner *ek* 'a, one,' then the relative clause must follow the head:

(99)  a.  Us  ne    ek  jhiil  dekhi  jo  bəhut  bəṛii  thii.
          he  INSTR  a   lake          wh  very   big    was
          "He saw a lake which was very big."

      b.  *jo  jhiil  bəhut  bəṛii  thii, us  ne  ek  dekhi

Finally, there is a restriction that nonrestrictive clauses such as those of (97a) can occur only in post-relative position, not as trailing or anticipatory relatives. Hence one has the following:

(100)  a.  *Ram  ne     ek  məkan  khəriida  jo  əmiir  hai.
           Ram   INSTR  a   house  bought    wh  rich   is

       b.  Us    admii  ne     ek  məkan  khəriida  jo  əmiir  hai.
           that  man    INSTR  a   house  bought    wh  rich   is

       c.  *Jo  ram  əmiir  hai  us  ne     ek  məkan  khəriida.
           wh  Ram  rich   is   he  INSTR  a   house  bought

       d.  Jo  admii  əmiir  hai  us  ne     ek  məkan  khəriida.
           wh  man    rich   is   he  INSTR  a   house  bought

I suspect that the constraint that anticipatory relatives require definite heads is universal. It holds in the other Indic languages (making certain allowances), and Hale suspects that it is also true of Warlpiri. Inasmuch as restrictive relatives with definite heads are generally 'old information', this may be related to the tendency for old information to appear first. Also, this construction might be related to the 'left dislocated' structures of such examples as *the guy who did that, I think he should be shot*.

1.1.3.4 *Sanskrit*: Inasmuch as the adjoined relative clause constructions do not have to form constituents with their heads, there is no reason why they should be restricted to having one head, or even one *wh* word.

Examples of multiple headed relative clauses may be found in Classical Sanskrit, such as the following:

(101) a. Yasya$_i$  yat$_j$     paitṛkam      ritkam          sa$_i$
who:GEN what:NOM paternal:NOM inheritance:NOM he:NOM
tad$_j$     gṛhnīta,   netaraḥ.
that:ACC should get not another
"Of whom what is the paternal inheritance, he should
get it and not somebody else."

b. Yenai     yāvān$_j$        yathā$_k$        'dharma
who:INSTR to what extent in what manner injustice
dharma  veha samīhitia, sai eva      tatphalam
justice or  is done   he exactly the fruits
            būnkte     tathāk     tāvadj            amutra
thereof will enjoy in that way to that extent in the
                vai.
other world indeed
"By whom to what extent [and] in what manner justice or
injustice is done, he will indeed enjoy the fruits
thereof to that extent [and] in that manner in the
other world."

In (101a) we have the *wh* relative words (the simple *ya*
series is used only as a relative pronoun, although more
complex forms built on *ya* have other uses) *yasya* and *yat*,
which are NP$_{rel}$ correlating with demonstratives *sa* and *tad*,
which are NP$_{hd}$ in the main clause. In (101b) the *wh* relative words are *yena*, *yāvān* and *yathā*, correlating with *sa*,
*tavad* and *tathā*.

If the reader, upon looking at these sentences, feels
at a loss as to how to interpret them, then there is a simple algorithm for constructing a paraphrase. Replace the *wh*
words with indefinites in *some*, and recast the relative
clause as a conditional. Thus one obtains: "if someone has
something as a paternal inheritance, then he should get it
and not someone else", "if someone does good or evil to some
extent in some way, then he shall enjoy the fruits thereof
in the next world to that extent and in that way".

I am informed that multiple headed relative clauses in
Sanskrit characteristically have this property of being
'generic' statements of laws. One might think, therefore,
to derive them from conditionals in some fashion. While
this might suffice in Sanskrit, we will find in Marathi
examples of multiple headed and multiple *wh*-worded relative
clauses which are not generic, but rather referential.

One might also think of associating the generic anticipatory relative clause with the anticipatory *wh-ever* clause

of English, exemplified in (102):

(102) Whoever steals my chickens, I'll set my dogs on him

We may note, however, that the *wh-ever* clause of English (a) allows only one *wh-ever* word (b) does not require a correlative definite in the matrix for every *wh-ever* word in the subordinate clause:

(103) *Whoever gives whatever to Lucy, she'll thank him for it.

(104) Whoever gets the job, I'll be displeased.

Structures like (104) are impossible for Sanskrit relative clauses.

1.1.3.5 *Marathi*:[8] Relativization in Marathi is roughly comparable to relativization in Sanskrit, but is made much more complex by the presence of a bewildering variety of alternative constructions. These are discussed by Junghare (1973). I will make no attempt to review them here, but will rather use the more straightforward constructions to exhibit a number of phenomena that are of theoretical interest.

Marathi is an SOV language with scrambling. It has postpositions and many following conjunctions, although some conjunctions, such as *ki* 'that', precede their clauses (as predicted by Kuno (1974), *ki* clauses are obligatorily extraposed to post-verbal position), and other words that correspond to conjunctions in English, such as *jər* 'if' and *jəri* 'although', may occur within their clauses as if they were adverbs.

There are four cases: nominative, dative-accusative, instrumental and genitive. The marker of the nominative is null. The dative-accusative has a marker *la* which is obligatory with humans, optional with animals, and omitted with inanimates. The marker of the instrumental is *ni*, and the genitive is marked by *c+Agr*, where Agr is a formative expressing the gender and number of the head N which the genitive NP modifies. The genitive marker takes the form *jha* when the possessed NP is masculine singular.

In intransitive sentences, of course, the subject is

nominative. In a transitive sentence in the present tense, the subject is nominative and the object is dative-accusative. In a transitive sentence in the past tense, the subject is instrumental, and the object remains in the dative-accusative. There is, finally, a construction taken by many 'psychological' verbs such as *awəṛ* 'like' in which the experiencer-of-affect takes the nominative. In this construction, the unmarked order is experiencer-object-verb: hence the dative-accusative is occupying the constituent structure position of the subject, and the nominative the position of the object. Verbs agree with their subjects and objects in person, gender and number in complex patterns which I will not describe.

We will be much concerned with the two determiners *j* 'wh' and *t* 'th'. Both may be used as determiners preceding their heads, or independently as pronouns. When used as pronouns, they take the case endings that would otherwise appear on the head N. Hence we have *ǰa muli-la* 'what girl-DA', *ǰa-la* 'who:FEM-DA'. *j* is used on $NP_{rel}$ of relative clauses, but not as an interrogative, and *t* is used as a demonstrative pronoun/definite article, as well as on the $NP_{hd}$ of relative clauses.

As in Hindi, we can find restrictive relative clauses preceding or following the matrix, $NP_{rel}$ marked with *j*, $NP_{hd}$ with *t*, and optional deletion of the head N of whichever NP comes first:

(105) a. Mĩ  ǰa muli-la pahili, mə-la ti (mulgi) awərte.
         I:INSTR wh girl-DA saw    I-DA th (girl) like
         "I like the girl who I saw".

   b. Mə-la ti mulgi awərte, mĩ  ǰa (muli)-la pahili
         I-DA th girl like    I:INSTR wh (girl)-DA saw
         "I like the girl who I saw".

The relative clauses in these examples illustrate the instrumental - dative-accusative construction in the past tense, and the matrices illustrate the dative-accusative - nominative construction with psychological verbs. The first, rather than the second instance of the head may be deleted under various circumstances which I do not understand and will not undertake to report.

Jungare (1973) analyses restrictive relative clauses as
being extracted from within the NP they modify, a view that
we have rejected for Warlpiri and Mabuiag, due to the
absence of any convincing evidence to support it.  In Sanskrit, we found evidence against the view in the form of
double and triple headed relative clauses, but the evidence
was weakened in the light of the fact that the clauses
receive an interpretation which makes them semantically
similar to conditionals.  I will exhibit referential multiple headed relative clauses in Marathi, but first I will
discuss a relation between the position of a relative
clause and its semantic interpretation.

The sentence *Ram thinks that the woman who is in the
kitchen is not in the kitchen* is said (see Postal 1974)
to have a reading in which a woman is in the kitchen and
Ram thinks that she is not in the kitchen, and a reading in
which Ram holds the contradiction that the woman who is in
the kitchen is not in the kitchen.  Following the philoso-
phical tradition, these readings are generally called the
transparent and the opaque readings, respectively.

In Marathi, these readings may be distinguished by the
positioning of the relative clause:  if it is placed
initial to the matrix clause, we get the transparent reading;  if it is placed initial to the complement clause we
get the contradictory opaque reading.  (106a) is the matrix
with no relative clause, (106b) has the relative clause
attached to the matrix to yield the transparent, coherent
reading, and in (106c) the relative clause is attached to
the complement to yield the contradictory opaque reading:

(106)  a.  Rama-la waṭṭe ki  ti bai  kičǝn  mǝdhe nahi.
           Ram-DA  thinks that th woman kitchen in    is not
           "Ram thinks that the woman is not in the kitchen."

       b.  Ji bai   kičǝn   mǝdhe ahe, Rama-la waṭṭe  ki   ti
           wh woman kitchen in    is   Ram-DA thinks that th
           (bai)  kičǝn  mǝdhe nahi.
           (woman) kitchen in    is not
           "Ram thinks that the woman who is in the kitchen is
           not in the kitchen (Transparent & Ram sane)"

```
c. Rama-la waṭṭe   ki   ǰi bai    kičən   mədhe ahe ti (bai)
   Ram-DA  thinks that wh woman kitchen in   is  th (woman)
   kičən   mədhe nahi.
   kitchen in    is not
   "Ram thinks that the woman who is in the kitchen is not
   in the kitchen (opaque & Ram crazy)"
```

Note that the relative clause goes between *ki* and the complement S, justifying the order of elements in the $\bar{S}$ $\longrightarrow$ COMP ($\bar{S}$) S ($\bar{S}$) rule.

This rule is further justified by the fact that two relative clauses cannot occur initially. Similarly, various sorts of adverbial clauses, such as conditionals in *jər...* *tər...* cannot cooccur initially with relative clauses, showing that they too occupy this slot:

```
(107) a. *Jo mulga kičən   mədhe ahe, ǰi bai    ajari ahe,
         wh boy    kitchen in   is   wh woman sick  is
         tya-ni         ti-la        mədət keli.
         th(masc)-INST th(fem)-DA help  did
         "The boy who is in the kitchen helped the woman who is
         sick."

      b. *Jər to ghora ǰinkel, jo mulga kičən   mədhe ahe, mĩ
         if th horse wins      wh boy    kitchen in   is   I:NOM
         tər tya-la       marin.
         then th(masc)-DA will hit
         "If that horse wins, then I will kill the boy who is
         in the kitchen."
```

Inasmuch as I later wish to relate *jər...tər* conditionals and related structures to relative clauses, this result is advantageous. I have not investigated the behaviour of trailing clauses, or of combinations of anticipatory and trailing clauses.

I now turn to multiple headed relatives. Below is a series of double headed relative clauses, the first three anticipatory, the last one trailing:

```
(108) a. Jo mulga ǰa muli-la pahato, *(tya) mula-la *(ti) mulgi
         wh boy   wh girl     sees      th    boy-DA  th  girl
         awərte.
         likes
         "The boy who sees the girl likes her."

      b. J̌a mula-ni   ǰa muli      dueš   kela tya-ni
         wh boy-INST wh girl-GEN hatred did  tha(masc)-INST
         ti-la       marli.
         th(fem)-DA killed
         "The boy who hated the girl killed her."
```

   c. J̌a mula-ni ǰa muli-la mərət keli, to       ti-la
      wh boy-INST wh girl-DA help  did   th(masc) th(fem)-DA
        marli
        killed
      "The girl who the boy helped liked him."

   d. Tya mula-ni  tya muli-la marli ǰa-ni       ǰi-ca
      th boy-INST  th  girl-DA killed wh(masc)-INST wh(fem)-GEN
        dueš   kela.
        hatred did
      "The boy who hated the girl killed her."

The translations given are ambiguous. The meanings of the examples are best given in logicalese. (108a), for example, means that for the unique ordered pair ($x$, $y$) where $x$ is a boy and $y$ is a girl and $x$ sees $y$, $x$ likes $y$; and similarly for the others. I believe that the translations given have these readings along with others.

Inasmuch as these examples are of considerable importance, it is worth mentioning that I have found them with three different speakers, the first of whom volunteered one in the course of a discussion of the Sanskrit examples in the previous subsection. He said that although referential multiple headed relatives were unnatural in Sanskrit, they were acceptable in his own language. I have tried (not very hard) with no success to elicit them in Bengali, and Keenan has tried with limited success to get them in Hindi (personal communication).

We may observe in (108a) that each $j$-word in the relative clause must have its corresponding $t$-word in the matrix. This shows that this relative clause construction really does involve multiple $NP_{rel}$-$NP_{hd}$ connections. Skepticism on this point may be further abated by observing that a multiple $j$-word relative clause may be used to answer a multiple $k$-word (interrogative) question:

  (109) Q: Konta mulga kontya muli berober dating kərto?
        which boy  which  girl with    dating does

     A: J̌a-la        ǰi     awərtę.
       wh(masc)-DA wh(fem) likes

     Q: "Which boy is dating which girl?"

     A: "who likes who."

The answer is presumably a reduced form of *jăla ǰi awəṛte,*
*to mulga tya muli berober dating kərto,* which is of the
same general form as the clauses of (108), except that pronominalization between NP$_{rel}$ and NP$_{hd}$ goes backwards.

These constructions have about them somewhat of the air
of Bach-Peters sentences. This is not surprising, inasmuch
as one of the more obvious ways to go about providing a
semantics for them would be to revise the device of the
'double NP' proposed by Keenan (1972, pp.458-459) to do the
semantics for Bach-Peters sentences.

I observed in the discussion of Hindi that a relative
clause could modify an indefinite NP if it followed the
matrix, but not if it preceded:

> (110) a. Mĩ    eka muli-la bheṭlə, mə-la ǰi (mulgi) awəṛte.
>           I:INST a  girl-DA met      I-DA wh  girl   like
>           "I met a girl who I like."
>
>       b. *Məla ǰi mulgi awəṛte, mĩ eka mulila bheṭlə.

Relative clauses following indefinite heads can also be
multiple headed:

> (111) Ek mulaga eka muli-la bheṭlə, ǰa-la       ǰi       awəṛte
>        a  boy    a  girl-DA met     wh(masc)-DA wh(fem) likes
>        "A boy met a girl and he likes her."

This construction has a flavour of 'afterthoughtiness'
about it, and we find that it cannot be used with interrogatives and indefinites that are controlled by negatives:

> (112) a. Tu  kona-la pahila?
>          you who-DA  saw
>          "Who did you see?"
>
>       b. *Tu  kona-la pahila jo ghorya-la marət hota?
>          you who-DA  saw    who horse-DA killing was
>
> (113) a. Mĩ      kunalahi    pahila nahi.
>          I:INST anybody(DA) saw    NEG
>          "I didn't see anybody."
>
>       b. *Mĩ      kunalahi    pahila nahi jo ghorya-la marət hota.
>          I:INST anybody(DA) saw    NEG  wh horse-DA killing was

This fact suggests that the clauses are in fact nonrestrictive, and this claim would follow from the general claim
made by Junghare that relative clauses without *to* are non-

restrictive.

Before leaving the subject of multiple headed relative clauses, I will mention the fact that Schwartz (1971) claimed that they existed in Telugu in a relative clause construction of the same general form as Indic. The construction was, of course, borrowed from Indic. Our observation of the type of structure was independent.

The anticipatory and trailing relative clause structures are also used to express various adverbial ideas. For example *jevha...tevha...* express *when...then...*, and *jithe...tithe...* express *where...there...* . Hence we have the following:

(114) a. Mĩ    jevha alo, tevha to joplela hota.
     I:INSTR when  came then  he sleeping was
     "When I arrived he was sleeping."

    b. To tevha dokya wər ubha     hota, jevha mĩ    alo.
     he then  head  on  standing was  when  I:INST came
     "He was standing on his head when I arrived."

(115) a. Jithe sawəli hoti, tithe Ram bəsla
     where shade  was   there Ram sat down
     "Where there was shade Ram sat down."

    b. Ram tithe bəsla,  jithe sawəli hoti.
     Ram there sat down where shade  was
     "Ram sat down where there was shade."

The anticipatory structure appears to be formally parallel with the English "when I arrived, then I sat down." I personally reject examples with *where...there...*, such as *where we found a four leaf clover, there we built a hut*, but this judgement is not universal.

Geis (1970) argued that adverbial clauses fell into two types: those related to relative clauses on nouns, such as *when* and *where* clauses, and those related to complement clauses on nouns, such as *if* and *although* clauses (consider the expressions *on the condition that...* and *in spite of the fact that...*). The evidence from Marathi undercuts this distinction. For not only do we have the abovementioned pairs, but also *jər...tər...* for *if...then...* and *jəri... təri...* for *although... in spite of that*. Hence corresponding to (114) and (115) we have (116) and (117):

(116) a. Jər to ithə yel, tər mi      tya-la goḷi   marin.
         if  he here comes then I:INST he-DA  bullet will kill
         "If he comes here, then I'll kill him."

      b. Mi    tər tya-la goḷi   marin,   to jər ithə yel.
         I:INST then he-DA  bullet will kill he if  here comes
         "If he comes here, then I'll kill him."

(117) a. Jəri     tya-ni majha kutrya-la marlə   təri
         although he-INST me:GEN dog-DA    killed "thalthough"
         mə-la to awəṛto.
         me-DA he likes
         "Although he killed my dog, in spite of that
         ("thalthough") I still like him."

      b. Mə-la təri      to awəṛto, majha kutrya-la jəri
         I-DA "thalthough" he likes  me:GEN dog        although
         marlə.
         killed
         "Although he killed my dog, in spite of that I still
         like him."

The fact that *jər*, *tər*, *jəri* and *təri* needn't occur clause
initially, but rather may occur fairly freely within their
clauses, suggests that they are not conjunctions (occupants
of COMP), but are rather like adverbs. *jevha, tevha, jithe*
and *tithe* appear to position themselves in roughly the same
way as do these other words.

We might still wish to dismiss this situation as a pure-
ly adventitious morphological paralellism, but there is
deeper evidence of a syntactic relation between *jər...tər...*
and *jəri...təri...* and the relative clause. Trailing relative clauses may have the appropriate *t*-word repeated after
them. Hence we have (118):

(118) To maṇus ajari ahe jo ithə kam  kərto to.
      th man   sick  is  wh here work does  th
      "The man who works here is sick."

Correspondingly we have the following examples with the
adverbial words:

(119) a. To tevha dokya wər obha      hota, jevha mĩ     alo
         he then  head  on  standing was   when  I:INST came
         tevha.
         then
         "When I came, then he was standing on his head."

      b. Ram tithe bəsla,  jithe sawəli hoti tithe.
         Ram there sat down where shade  was  there
         "Ram sat down where there was shade."

c. Mə-la təri           to awəṛto, jəri       majha kutrya-la
   me-DA "thalthough" he likes    although my      dog-DA
   marlə təri.
   killed "thalthough"

d. Mĩ       tər tya-la sangin     jər mĩ      tya-la bheṭlo
   I:INST then he-DA  will tell if  I:INST he-DA  meet
   tər.
   then

'if' and 'although' in Marathi thus seem closely related to
the relative clause construction in this language.

The problem raised by these examples is that it is difficult to think of how a smenatics of the sort that one
might envision for relative clauses would extend in any
straightforward way to these 'conjunctions'. I will venture
the suggestion that perhaps treating the conjunctions with
explicit quantification over possible worlds in a fashion
suggested, but not explained, by Postal (1974) would provide a satisfactory solution.

In English, also, we can find relative-like conjunctions.
Consider first that the *if* in the *if...then...* construction
is also used as a wh-word in indirect questions: *I don't
know if he will come.* Second, observe that *as...so...* form
a clearly correlative pair in *as ye sow, so shall ye reap*
and other examples of that ilk. Now in poetry and elevated
prose we may find *as...so...* pairs which are not ordinary
relative pronouns, but rather relate a clause giving grounds
to one giving the consequence, in a construction that is a
non-adversative counterpart to the Marathi *jəri...təri* construction. An example of this usage is the following pas-
sage from T.S.Eliot's "Little Gidding":

> But, as the passage now presents no hindrance
>   To the spirit unappeased and peregrine
>   Between two worlds become much like each other,
> So I find words I never thought to speak
>   On streets I never thought I should revisit
> When I left my body on a distant shore.

To conclude the discussion, we have shown that Marathi
relative clauses may have multiple *wh* words and multiple
heads, thus scotching any hope for a universal derivation
of relative clauses from clauses forming a constituent with
their head. We have shown some differences between antici-

patory and trailing clauses, and we have claimed that
lurking among the straightforward relative clauses are a
class of clauses that from conventional treatments of
semantics one would not expect to betray significant syntactic relations to relative clauses.  Marathi is clearly
a language worthy of further investigation.

1.1.3.6 *Navajo:*  In this section, I will give more thorough
consideration to the extraposed relative clause in Navajo,
and will contrast it with the extraposed relative in English.  The Navajo material here is drawn from Perkins
(1975).

The extraposed relative in English obeys the constraint
(with various sorts of loopholes, most of which I shall
ignore) that the head and the relative clause cannot be
separated by another NP.  Hence while (120) is acceptable,
(121) is not ambiguous:

(120)  A woman came in who was tall.

(121)  A boy kissed a girl who was tall.

In Navajo, on the other hand, there is no such constraint.
Hence (122a) is doubly, and (122b) triply ambiguous:

(122)  a.  Ashkii at'ééd yoo'į       hashtl'izh
           boy    girl  3:PROG:3:see mud
           yiih-yítlizh-éę.
           3:in-PERF:3:fall-REL
           "The boy who fell in the mud sees the girl."
           "The boy sees the girl who fell in the mud."

       b.  Ashkii at'ééd łįį' ye-inílóóz       ba'níłtsood-éę.
           boy    girl  horse 3:to-3:PERF:3:led 3:PERF:1:feed-REL
           "The boy whom I have fed led the horse to the girl."
           "The boy led the horse to the girl whom I have fed."
           "The boy led the horse which I have fed to the girl."

This Navajo extraposed relative is less restricted than
the English in yet another fashion.  Extraposition rules in
English are subject to an ironclad constraint against
extracting elements from subject clauses.  Hence we have
(123):

(123)  a.  That a woman has arrived who knows French is good.

       b.  *That a woman has arrived is good who knows French.

In Navajo, we find these data exactly reversed:

(124) a. \*ɫééchąą'í iisxį́-nígíí    ba'niɫtsood-ę́ę    yá'át'ééh.
        dog       PERF:3:kill-REL 3:PERF:1:feed-REL it is good
        "It is good that the dog which I have fed has killed
        something."

     b. ɫééchąą'í iisxį́-nígíí     yá'át'ééh ba'niɫtsood-ę́ę.
        dog       PERF:3:kill-REL it is good 3:PERF:1:feed-REL

(124a), in which the relative clause *ba'niɫtsoodę́ę* 'which I
have fed' has been extraposed to the end of the subject
complement *ɫééchąą'í iisxį́nígíí* 'that the dog has killed
something', is ungrammatical. (124b), where the extraposition has proceeded to the end of the sentence, is
acceptable. The ungrammaticality of (124a) I shall deal
with later. For the present, let us meditate on the acceptable (124b) in contrast to the English examples (123).

    Ross (1967), on the basis of a variety of evidence,
including sentences like (123), arrived at the following
proposed constraint on transformational application (Ross
1967, ex. 5.58):

    (125)   Any rule whose structural index is of the form ...A Y,
          and whose structural change specifies that A is to be
          adjoined to the right of Y, is upward bounded.

However, there is another constraint proposed by Ross that
can explain (123), the Sentential Subject Constraint (Ross
1967, ex. 4.254):

    (126)   *The Sentential Subject Constraint:*

          No element dominated by an S may be moved out of that
          S if that node S is dominated by a node NP which is
          itself immediately dominated by S.

The reader may observe that the crucial evidence in the
discussion that motivates (125) (sections 5.1.1.-5.1.2.)
is all explicable by the Sentential Subject Constraint. We
have for example the following pairs:

    (127)   a.  That it was obvious that Bob was lying is not true.

           b.  \*That it was obvious is not true that Bob was lying.
              (5.18)

    (128)   a. A proof that the claim had been made that John had
            lied was given.

     b. *A proof that the claim had been made was given that
       John had lied.  (2.9)

(129) a. That Sam didn't pick those packages up which are to
       be mailed tomorrow is possible. (5.22c)

     b. *That Sam didn't pick those packages up is is
       possible which are to be mailed tomorrow (5.21)

(130) a. That a review came out yesterday of this article
       is catastrophic. (5.55a)

     b. *That a review came out yesterday is catastrophic
       of this article. (5.55b)

These examples illustrate the phenomenon with ordinary
Extraposition, Extraposition of Relative Clauses and Complements from NP and Extraposition of PP.

Let us try to construct a series of examples testing for
(125) (which I shall henceforth call the Right Roof Constraint) in examples where the Sentential Subject Constraint
does not interfere:

(131) a. ?*Bill said that it would be difficult in his
       memorandum to get the project funded.

     b. ?*You promised that a person would come on the
       telephone who would fix the refrigerator.

     c. **He admitted that the hypothesis had been
       disconfirmed in his paper that quarks were
       the major ingredient in baby food.

     d. ?*You said that a man would come today yesterday
       who would fix the faucet.

     e. ?*The professor announced that he had stolen a
       vase in class from the most closely guarded
       temple in India.

These are all rather bad, but they hardly constitute an
overwhelming battery of evidence, and to my ear they are
not as bad as the (b) examples of (127-130).

If an alternative explanation for (131) can be worked
out, which wouldn't surprise me (perhaps on the basis of
their ungainly constituent structure), then it might be
possible to remove the Right Roof Constraint from the
grammar of English.  In light of Perkins' and Kaufman's
work on Navajo, and Satyanarayana and Subbarao's (1973)
work on Hindi and Telugu, this would constitute an advance.

(124b) requires not only that there be no Right Roof
Constraint in Navajo, but also that there be no Sentential

Subject Constraint.  Happily, this has already been suggested on independent grounds.  (Platero 1974, pp.xx) suggests
that Navajo relativization does not obey a Sentential Subject Constraint, but instead suffers from an idiolectally
varying disability against relativizing into nominal complements.  The extraposition process discussed by Perkins
would appear to be immune from this disability.

Perkins gives examples that show that a relative clause
may be extracted from several clauses deep, but may not be
left at the end of any of the intervening clauses.  Hence
we have the acceptable (133a), and the series of failed
variants (133b, c):

(133)  a.  Łééchąą'í biładideeshdǫǫł nisin  dishní
           dog        3:FUT:1:shoot   1:want PERF:1:say
           shishxash-ę́ę.
           1:PERF:3:bite-REL
           "I said that I wanted to shoot the dog that bit me."

       b.  *Łééchąą'í biładideeshdǫǫł shishxashę́ę nisin dishní.

       c.  *Łééchąą'í biładideeshdǫǫł nisin shishxashę́ę dishní.

Perkins further observes that although a relative clause
can be extraposed from within a sentential subject, one
cannot be extraposed from within a relative clause or a
coordinated NP:

(134)  a.  Łééchąą'í nahał'in-ę́ę    dóó mási ahigá.
           dog        IMP:3:bark-REL and cat  RECIP:IMP:3:fight
           "The dog that was barking and the cat are fighting."

       b.  *Łééchąą'í dóó mási ahigá nahałinę́ę.

(135)  a.  Hastiin dibé ba'níłtsood-ę́ę    neis'áh-ę́ę
           man     sheep 3:PERF:1:feed-REL 3:PERF:3:butcher-REL
           adeeshgizh.
           REFL:PERF:3:cut
           "The man who butchered the sheep which I have fed cut
           himself."

       b.  *Hastiin dibé heis'áhę́ę adeeshgizh ba'níłtsoodę́ę.

We are thus confronted with what appears to be an argument
that Navajo actually has a rule extraposing relative clauses
from their heads:  some, although not all, of the island
constraints are obeyed, and we could explain the requirement
that the extraposed clause wind up at the end of sentence by

having the extraposition rule be a root transformation.

Nonetheless, mortal counterevidence to this picture exists. Perlmutter and Ross (1970) observed the following sentence pattern in English:

(136)  A man came in and a woman went out who were similar.

I proposed in the introduction to this chapter that this example had the deep structure (3). The fact that the predicate of the relative clause requires a plural subject prevents it from being derived by Extraposition and Right Node Raising from a pair of relative clauses, one in each conjunct.

We can find examples of this form in Navajo:

(137)  Ashkii yah 'íiyá    dóó at'ééd ch'in-íiyá
       boy   into PERF:3:go and girl  out-PERF:3:go
       ałhinoolin'-ę́ę.
       RECIP:3:look like-REL
       "A girl came in and a boy went out who were similar."

We can also find in Navajo examples of a form impossible in English. In English, the two heads for the relative clause have to be in different conjuncts of a coordinate clause. Hence we cannot say (138):

(138)  *The dog is chasing the cat which were fighting.

But the corresponding structure is perfectly acceptable in Navajo.

(139)  Łééchąą'i mási yinoołchééł    ahigán-ę́ę.
       dog       cat  3:PROG:3:chase RECIP:IMP:3:fight-REL
       "The dog is chasing the cat which were fighting."

In light of the Navajo, it is the *(138) of English that is problematical. I would propose that the explanation for *(138) is the same as the explanation for the non-ambiguity of (121). The nonambiguity of (121) shows that there is in English a constraint preventing there from being an NP intervening between a relative clause and its head. This principle would prevent *which were fighting* from taking *dog* as a head in (139) due to the intervention of *cat*. Failure of number agreement then renders the example ungrammatical. Navajo, which lacks this constraint, thus has ambiguity in sentence patterns corresponding to (121) and allows sentence patterns like (139).

Why doesn't the constraint on intervention block (136)? This is presumably a consequence of the general nature of 'Across-the-board' phenomena in coordinate structures. For the present, I shall merely say that when the constraint is presented with a coordination of structures, it applies in each conjunct individually, and not to the coordinate structure as a whole. This proposal predicts that (140) should be unambiguous:

(140) A man saw a woman and a boy saw a girl who were similar.

The relative clause should modify *woman* and *girl*. As best as I can tell, this prediction is borne out.

The proposal that extraposed relatives in Navajo are base-generated in the position they occupy in surface structure appears to contradict the testimony of the evidence that there is a root transformation of Extraposition that obeys island constraints. We can explain why a relative clause can only be extraposed to the end of the main clause by noting that Navajo is absolutely rigid in its requirement that any subordinate clause end with the verb of that clause. Platero (1974) notes processes that may extrapose the subject of a main clause to the end of the clause beyond the verb, but these possibilities of movement are completely absent in subordinate clauses. By imposing the surface requirement that a subordinate clause end with its verb, we may account for the apparent evidence that Extraposition is a root transformation.

Now for the island constraints. Bresnan (1974b) attacks the notion that island constraints constitute diagnostics for movement by showing that they constrain a deletion rule. I propose that these facts from Navajo be taken as evidence that island constraints apply between elements that are related by no transformational rule at all, but rather are connected by the sorts of extra-constituent structure relations that I have been suggesting to hold between heads, relative nouns and complementizers of relative clauses. The ungrammatical (134b) would thus have the structure (141):

(141)

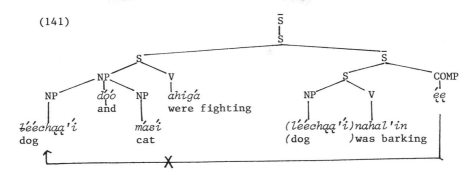

The spot is marked with an X where the Complementizer-Head
Connection crosses the coordinate structure boundary.

The reader will note the presence of one assumption
that is from the point of view of the Navajo quite gratui-
tous:  I have assumed that the Navajo extraposed relative
is introduced by a rule S → S S̄.  The purpose of this
assumption is to create a structural paralellism between
the English and the Navajo extraposed relatives.

There are two considerations that motivate introducing
extraposed relatives in English with S → S S̄ rather than
with any of the other alternatives one might imagine.  First
the construction can stack:

(142)   A woman came in who I knew who had taught at Berkeley.

Second, consider what happens when we attach an extraposed
relative to a complement sentence:

(143)   It is obvious that a man came in and (*that) a woman
        went out who were similar.

By introducing the relative clause as an expansion of S
rather than of S̄, we explain why the conjunction *that* cannot
be repeated on the second conjunct.  I believe that when
the sense of the relative clause is such that a derivation
by Right Node Raising from multiple relative clauses in a
coordinate structure is possible, then the conjunction may
be repeated:

(144)   It is obvious that a man came in and that a woman
        went out who were wearing boots.

Why should the English and the Navajo structures be
assimilated?  They both appear to be in some sense 'variants'

of an embedded relative clause structure. In this feature, they are distinguished from the trailing relative clauses of the Australian and Indic languages we have observed above. They have in addition the property of not corresponding to any anticipatory relative clause structure.

Next, we observed in section 1.1.2.1 that extraposed relatives in Navajo obligatorily underwent a rule deleting $NP_{rel}$. In English, similarly, the $NP_{rel}$ of an extraposed relative clause must be a relative pronoun or it must be deleted (assuming with Bresnan (1970) that English that-relative clauses suffer deletion of $NP_{rel}$). In contra-distinction, we see that in the trailing relative clauses of the previous subsections, $NP_{rel}$ could be repeated. I hypothesize that obligatory deletion or pronominalization of $NP_{rel}$ is a restriction which may be imposed on relative clauses introduced by rules of the form $X \longrightarrow X \bar{S}$ or $X \longrightarrow \bar{S} X$ (where X is any category), but not on relative clauses introduced by other sorts of rules, such as $\bar{S} \longrightarrow COMP (\bar{S}) S (\bar{S})$ or $CP \longrightarrow NP (\bar{S})$ CASE. We are thus led to predict that nonrestrictive relatives in English can have full NP heads, which is indeed the case:

> (145) My dog, which faithful animal has guarded me for years, is waiting outside your door.

We might further ask why it seems to be that anticipatory relatives never seem to require pronominalization or deletion of $NP_{rel}$: under the present approach, we may propose that it is because there is no rule of the form $S \longrightarrow \bar{S} S$ in any language. Of course this fact itself requires explanation.

I finally observe that adjoined, but not extraposed relative clauses may have multiple *wh* words. Hence *a man came in and a woman went out who loved who* is bad in English, and there is no Navajo sentence for "*a dog was chasing the cat which bit which." Perhaps this fact is related to the pronominalization requirement noted above.

I therefore propose that there is a type of relative clause, the extraposed relative, which is essentially a variant of the embedded relative and is quite different

from the trailing relative. Extraposed relatives are in-
troduced by the rule S $\longrightarrow$ S $\bar{\text{S}}$. That the Navajo extraposed
relative is introduced by this rule is at present more of
a prediction than a fact.

1.1.3.7 *Remarks on Multiple Headedness:* We may observe
that the multiple headed clauses we have seen fall into
two types: those where a single $NP_{rel}$ has multiple antecedents, and cases where a single relative clause has multiple $NP_{rel}$, each with its own antecedent. This latter case
I hypothesize to be impossible with relative clauses intro-
duced by rules of the form $X \longrightarrow X \bar{\text{S}}$ and $X \longrightarrow \bar{\text{S}} X$.

We are led to suspect that multiple *wh* words may be possible with nonrestrictive relatives in English. The following, suggested by Bill Cantrall, is as good as they come:

(146)  ??I scribbled on the cover of a book, which cover
       of which was orange.

All examples that I can construct are rather dubious, but
often less so than one might expect. Note that (146),
unlike the relatives of 1.1.3.6, requires a comma pause
before the relative clause, making it a sort of nonrestrictive.

Finally, the existence of multiple headed clauses
necessitates complications in the abstract relations I have
proposed to be involved in relative clauses. In chapter 2,
I will cast a proposal in more rigorous terms, but here I
will describe a scheme that lets us retain the graphic
representation we have been using without too much difficulty. Let us say that COMP of a relative clause expands
into an n-tuple $R^n$. Each R may then be connected by arrows
to a single $NP_{rel}$ and to a nonnull set of $NP_{hd}$. In all
English $R^n$, we have n=1 (with the dubious exception of such
examples as (146)), but in Marathi we may have n=2, 3, etc.
Sentence (107a) will thus receive the representation (147)
on the following page. This expansion of COMP into an
n-tuple will offend most readers, and when we move to a
more abstract form of representation we shall eliminate it.

Before closing section 1.1, I would like to mention one
final fact. It appears that in all cases, the heads of a

82

(147)

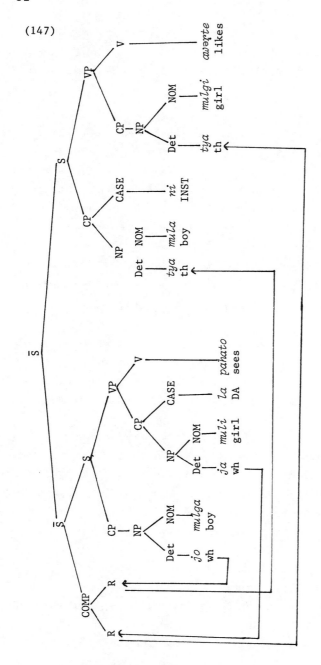

For the unique pair $(x, y)$ where $x$ is a boy, $y$ is a girl and
$x$ sees $y$, $x$ likes $y$.

relative clause are in construction with that clause, in
the sense of Klima (1964).  We may easily accommodate this
with a principle restricting configurations of trees-cum-
abstract relations.  Such a principle, along with many
others, will be given in chapter 2.

1.2  *The treatment of* $NP_{rel}$:  In this section, I shall discuss the various things that happen to $NP_{rel}$.  I shall
first in 1.2.1 discuss languages in which $NP_{rel}$ bears a
special morphological mark, but is not deleted by a special
process or moved to the front of the clause.  In one of
these languages, $NP_{rel}$ is replaced by a special pronoun,
and in the other, a special agreement marker is placed on
the verb, which may be regarded as a copy of a specially
marked pronoun that subsequently deletes by ordinary pronominalization processes.  In 1.2.2 I will discuss some
languages in which $NP_{rel}$ is simply deleted, and in 1.2.3 I
will discuss the preposing of $NP_{rel}$ to the front of the
relative clause.  Finally, in 1.2.4 I will give some general
discussion of constraints on the form and position of $NP_{rel}$.

1.2.1  *Languages marking* $NP_{rel}$:  I will here discuss two
languages with marking but not preposing of $NP_{rel}$:  Crow
and Swahili.  Crow is a transparent case of the phenomenon
inasmuch as in the construction we shall discuss there is a
special pronoun that takes the place of $NP_{rel}$.  We require
an analysis to arrive at the conclusion that Swahili has
marking without movement of $NP_{rel}$.

1.2.1.1 *Crow*:  Crow is a Siouan language with about (very
roughly) 4,000 speakers, spoken in southeastern Montana.  It
is an SOV language with postpositions and following conjunctions and complementizers, and considerable scrambling.
The person and number of subjects, objects and possessors
are extensively marked on verbs, postpositions and possessed
NP.  A particularly interesting feature of the language is a
rich array of determiners on NP which are homophonous with
and semantically similar or identical to "complementizers"
that appear on verbs.  The orthography used is that adopted
by the Crow Bilingual Education Project.  Dale Oldhorn,

George Reed and Rose Chesarek have been especially helpful
in providing me with information about Crow, although many
other members of the Crow Tribe have been of assistance.

Crow has at least four relative clause constructions,
an internal head relative, an anticipatory relative, a
post-relative and a free relative. My knowledge of the
language is too small to allow me to say much insightful
about most of these. I will therefore make some points
which are of general interest with the post-relative
structure, then briefly describe the others.

In the postrelative construction, the head NP takes the
determiner -m and the relative clause takes the termination
e:s, which serves as an anaphoric definite article on NP,
and is attached to clauses representing old, "presupposed"
information. $NP_{rel}$ is represented by the word ak, which
functions only as a subject. We thus attain the NP (148):

> (148)  shiká:ka-m ak bi:-lich-é:sh.
>       boy-SPEC  who me-hit-DEF
>       "The boy who hit me."

I gloss -m as SPEC because it generally makes NP specific.
So shiká:ke aw-áka:-ssa:-k 'boy I-see-NEG-DECL', 'I didn't
see any boy', but shiká:kam awaká:ssa:k 'I didn't see a
(specific) boy.' k is a formative that ends declarative
clauses.

We may determine that ak is a syntactically motile word
rather than merely an agentive nominalization prefix by
observing that it may occur freely with a relative clause
containing several major constituents:

> (149)  a.  shiká:ka-m ak hú:le:sh  Bill-sh dich-é:sh
>            boy-SPEC  who yesterday Bill-NM hit-DEF
>
>       b.  shiká:kam hú:le:sh ak Billsh diché:sh
>
>       c.  shiká:kam hú:le:sh Billsh ak diché:sh
>            "The boy who hit Bill yesterday."

The sh formative that I gloss NM is, I believe, a form of
the definite article that is attached to proper names.

ak may appear within a subordinate clause in the
relative clause. Hence we get (150):

(150) Shiká:ka-m Bill-sh ak hu:wía-:-k hilía:ch-e:sh
boy-SPEC Bill-NM who come-will-DECL think-DEF
"The boy who Bill thinks will come."

There is a constraint in English that if a relative
clause has a subject and a complement clause containing NP
coreferential to the subject, then the subject can be $NP_{rel}$,
but none of the NP in the complement clause may. This
phenomenon along with others is subsumed under the Crossover
Principles of Postal (1971, 1972). Hence we have the data
of (151):

(151) a. the boy $who_i$ thought $he_i$ was smart

b. the boy $who_i$ $he_j$ thought was smart

c. *the boy $who_i$ $he_i$ thought was smart

Postal (1971) proposed accounting for this with a constraint
on movement: the movement of the pronoun *who* in (151c)
over the coreferential pronoun *he* was to block the sentence.
In the (1972) paper, he suggested retreating from this
position. The data from Crow show that this retreat was
well-advised, inasmuch as this relative clause construction
obeys the constraint even though $NP_{rel}$ is not moved at all,
but merely assumes a special form. If we intercalate *ak*
between an NP that its appropriate as an object of the complement verb and the complement verb, we prevent it from
being analysed as a constituent of the topmost S in the
relative clause. Then we get the following:

(152) a. shiká:ka-m ak ú:xa-m dappeé-k hilía:ch-e:sh
boy-SPEC who deer-SPEC kill-DECL think-DEF
"The boy who thinks he killed a deer."

b. shiká:ka-m ú:xa-m ak dappeé-k hilía:ch-e:sh
boy-SPEC deer-SPEC who kill-DECL think-DEF
"The boy $who_i$ $he_j$ thinks killed a deer."

*"The boy $who_i$ thinks $he_i$ killed a deer."

I shall now briefly run through the other constructions.
In the internal head relative clause, $NP_{rel}$ ends in *-m* or
nothing, and the complementizer may be at least *e:sh* or
nothing, and possibly others, such as *m*, as well. We have
for example (153):

    (153) a.  Mary-sh shiká:ka-m hi:-lich-é:sh
              Mary-NM boy-SPEC   meet-sort of-DEF
              "The boy who Mary is dating."

          b.  Mary-sh shiká:ke hi:-lich-é:sh
              Mary-NM boy       meet-sort of-DEF
              "The boy who Mary is dating."

$NP_{rel}$ may occupy many positions within the relative clause -
subject, object, possessor, etc., and it may be in many
kinds of subordinate clauses, such as conditionals and
indirect questions. This construction thus makes up for
the restricted nature of the *ak* postrelative.

There appears to be an anticipatory relative in which a
clause ending in *e:sh* precedes the matrix. The $NP_{rel}$ take
*m* and the $NP_{hd}$ take the demonstrative *koó*. I consider the
analysis of this structure as a real relative clause highly
speculative:

    (154)  Shiká:ka-m bú:bchi-m bía:ka:ta-m kush-shí:ch-e:sh koó
           boy-SPEC    ball-SPEC girl-SPEC   to-throw-DEF     DEM
           shiká:ke koo bú:bche koó bía:ka:te ak-dichi-k.
           boy      DEM DEM      girl     with-hit-DECL
           "Ya know the boy who threw the ball at the girl? Well,
           he hit her with it."

There are finally the free relatives. These occur in
four varieties. When relativising on the subject, one uses
*ak*. When relativising on objects, one uses the pronoun *ba:(m)*
'something' to replace $NP_{rel}$. Adverbial clauses of place,
time and manner are formed with *ala* replacing $NP_{rel}$. These
three constructions are illustrated in the following:

    (155) a.  Bill-sh ak  dapp-é:sh sahí:-k.
              Bill-NM who kill-DEF  Cree-DECL
              "The one who killed Bill was a Cree."

          b.  Ba:      aw-áke xawí:-k.
              something I-see  bad-DECL
              "What I saw was bad."

          c.  Ú:xa-m      an-dá:-ppe, al ú:xam dá:ppe.
              deer-SPEC ADV-you-kill
              "The time, manner or place in which you killed a deer."

The final construction is that used when $NP_{rel}$ is an instrumental. Crow treats instrumental NP in a very special way:
between the instrumental NP and the verb occurs a formative
*i:* which may come anywhere between major constituent breaks.

Hence we get the following:

(156)  a. Bas-í:la:le i:    b-ilápxe  chichúche kuss-a:wa:lé:-k.
          my-car       INST my-father Hardin    to    I:take-DECL
          "I took my father to Hardin in my car."

       b. Basí:la:le bilápxe i: chichúche kussa:wa:lé:k.

       c. Basí:la:le bilápxe chichúche i:kussa:wa:lé:k

Of these variants, (a) and (c) are the best.  To get a
relative clause on an instrumental, one merely takes the
clause, keeping *i:* and omitting NP$_{rel}$, supplying the appropriate complementizer (most often null) to the verb.  Hence
one gets *i:lia:-we* 'with do-I', 'what I did it with.'  It
is worth mentioning that free relative clauses are a very
productive source of common nouns: from the relative clause
of (157a) comes the noun *amma:ia:schilua:* 'store', and from
that of (157b) comes *i:wa:wara:tua:* 'pencil':

(157)  a. am-ma:-ía:schil-ua:
          ADV-something-buy-Pl
          "Where one buys things."

       b. i:-wa:-wara:t-úa:
          INST-something-write-Pl
          "What one writes with."

The Pl is an agreement marker for a third person plural
subject that is deleted, which expresses indefinite agency.
Hence we have *dit-ú:-k* (hit-Pl-DECL) "they killed him (with
the indefinite agency use of 'they')."  We can spot the
nouns because they, unlike relative clauses, can pluralize.
Hence we have *amma:ía:schiluo* 'stores', *i:wa:wara:túo*
'pencils.'

   I am reasonably sure that the construction with *ba:*
cannot be used with a head.  The evidence with *ala* is
rather contradictory.  Although Crows seem to overwhelming-
ly reject examples that I concoct with *ala* in a postrelative structure, they will occasionally let one by.  I have
found no way to tell whether the instrumental construction
appears in a postrelative structure, for the reason that
a sequence such as 'pencil letter *i:-* I wrote' could be
analysed either as a postrelative or an internal head
relative.

In Crow, we thus find a clear case of replacement of
NP$_{rel}$ by a special pronoun, and a variety of further
structures which demand more thorough investigation.

1.2.1.2 *Swahili*:  The Swahili construction may be regarded
as a variation on the Crow.  Unlike the Crow *ak* construction, NP$_{rel}$ may occupy almost any grammatical position.
Also unlike Crow, NP$_{rel}$ gets deleted, presumably by the
ordinary pronoun dropping rules.  But the special mark on
NP$_{rel}$ leaves a trace in the form of a special agreement
marking on the verb.

I shall give much more background information about
Swahili than about the other languages in this study, since
with this information, we can solve an interesting problem.

1.2.1.2.1 *NP*:  Swahili has an intricate noun-class system.
For each class, there are two characteristic prefixes (one
or both of them sometimes null), a singular and a plural,
which are attached to all occurrences of the noun itself.
Hence we have *m-tu, wa-tu* 'man, men'; *ki-tabu, vi-tabu*,
'book, books'; *yai, ma-yai* 'egg, eggs.'  Furthermore, corresponding to each number/class prefix, there is a 'concord'
which is added to words bearing various syntactic relations
to the NP, and thus causes them to agree with it.  Verbs
take a concord which indicates the class/number of their
subject: *m-tu a-tatosha, wa-tu wa-tatosha* 'the man will be
sufficient, the men will be sufficient'; *ki-tabu ki-tatosha,
vi-tabu vi-tatosha* 'the book will be sufficient, the books
will be sufficient'; *yai li-tatosha, ma-yai ya-tatosha* 'the
egg will be sufficient, the eggs will be sufficient.'
Concords are also added to adjectives modifying nouns, both
predicate and attributive.

For animate beings, there is a set of personal pronouns,
1st, 2nd and 3rd persons, singular and plural.  The first
and second persons function like special noun-classes,
having their own concord affixes, while the 3rd person uses
the concord for animates (the *m-tu - wa-tu* class).  One has
hence *mimi ni-takufa* 'I will die'; *yeye a-takufa* 'he will
die.'  Since most pronouns have some concord prefix referencing them, the pronouns are freely deletable when non-

emphatic. For inanimates there are no surface pronouns at all: one must make do with concord prefixes, demonstratives and NP such as *kitu* 'thing.'

There are some demonstratives which can be used either as determiners or as independent pronouns. The demonstratives are built from a stem *-le* or *h-* with a concord which is usually similar to that used on verbs to agree with the subject. For the *-le* demonstrative, which means 'that, yonder,' one merely prefixes the appropriate concord: *m-tu yu-le* 'that man,' *ma-yai ya-le* 'those eggs.' The *h-* demonstrative is built by first suffixing to *h-* the vowel of the concord, and then the whole concord itself: *m-tu h-u-yu* 'this man,' *wa-tu h-u-wa* 'these men,' *ki-tabu h-i-ki* 'this book,' *yai h-i-li* 'this egg,' *ma-yai h-a-ya* 'these eggs.' Another demonstrative, supposedly used only to refer to things which have already been mentioned, is formed by suffixing an *o* to the end of the *h-* demonstrative. The *o* causes phonological changes leading to such things as *mtu huyo*, *watu hao*, *kitabu hicho*, etc.

One of the most interesting grammatical categories in Swahili is the locative. Swahili locatives are characteristically used to express adverbial thematic relations such as place and time, but they can also be used as surface and even underlying subjects. One locative is the noun *mahali* 'place.' This takes its own special concord *pa*, and one hence gets such sentences as *mahali pa-le pa-meharibika* 'that place has been spoiled.'

More interesting locatives are made from nouns by suffixing *-ni*. One hence has *mji-ni* 'in the town,' *nyumba-ni* 'in the house,' *mlango-ni* 'at the door.' The locatives behave syntactically like NP. Although the locatives themselves lack any class-prefix other than that of the NP they are built from, the concords on the elements agreeing with them show that they fall into three classes, depending on the kind of locative relation they express. The concords are *m(u)* 'within,' *pa* 'at' and *ku* 'around, along' (meanings grossly oversimplified). Demonstratives are built from the locative concords, and one has thus such expressions as

*m-le (sanduku-nu)* 'in there (in the box),' *h-a-pa mlango-ni*
'there at the door,' and so forth.

In locative expressions with definite subjects ('the
animals are in the forest'), the verb *to be* (usually phonologically null) is used with the subject concord of the
subject preceding the verb, and the locative concord of the
locative following the verb, followed by the *o* which was
mentioned above. One has hence *ki-su k-ko (<ku-o) nymbani*
'the knife is in the house,' *kisu ki-po (<pa-o) mezani*
'the knife is on the table,' and *kisu ki-mo (<mu-o) sanduku-
ni* 'the knife is in the box.'

There are two prepositions, *kwa* and *na*, which frequently
have their objects copied onto them in the form of the
concord+*o* combination we have seen several times before.
For brevity, I will refer to this combination of concord+*o*
as a kihusiano (pl. vihusiano), a term invented by a native
grammarian. For each noun-class and number (including the
locatives) there is a class-prefix (frequently null), concord affixes and a kihusiano. For one class, the *m-tu* class
(singular animate) the kihusiano is irregular, being *ye*,
which, interestingly enough, turns out to be the stem from
which the third person singular personal pronoun *yeye* is
formed. Hence we frequently copy vihusiano onto *kwa* and *na*,
getting such forms as *naye* 'with him.' For 1st and 2nd
person pronouns, the base from which the pronoun is formed
by reduplication is copied onto *na*. Hence one has *mimi*,
*nami* 'me, with me.' In the third person plural, the pronoun is *wao*, and the kihusiano is *o*, a contraction of *wao*.

The preposition *na* is primarily comitative and instrumental; hence *nacho* 'with it (say, a book), *nayo* 'with
them (eggs).' *kwa* is generally agentive and instrumental;
*kwao* 'by them (people).'

There is thus a rule copying underlying pronouns onto
these prepositions in the form of a kihusiano. When the
object of the preposition is a full NP, the copying generally does not occur: hence *na fimbo* 'with a stick.' The
copying rule assures that *na* and *kwa* are never left stranded
without any expression of their object, since precisely the

things that get deleted freely, nonemphatic pronouns, get copied obligatorily.

1.2.1.2.2  Non-Relative Verbs:  The Swahili verb is composed by adding prefixes and suffixes to the stem.  The suffixes express for the most part categories of voice which are not my concern in this paper.  The prefixes may be regarded as clitics which have become one word with the stem.  They fit into the following five slots:

(158)  Pre-Verbal Clitic Slots:

| I | II | III | IV | V |
|---|---|---|---|---|
| *ha* | subject | tense/ | relative | object |
| | concord | aspect, | kihusiano | concord |
| (negation) | | *si* (neg) | | |

In this subsection I will discuss slots I, II, III and V, leaving IV for the discussion of relativization.  Slots II and V are well behaved, their contents varying independently of each other (excepting some twitches caused by relativization).  I, III and IV have mutual interdependencies. The prefix *ha-* (in certain forms supplemented with the suffix *-i*) is used to make negatives.  It is used only with certain tense-aspects, and never when there is a relative kihusiano present.  *ha* is never followed by the subject concord *ni* 'I'.  Instead the sequence *ha-ni* is suppletively replaced by *si* (distinct from the negative *si* of slot III).

The occupants of slot III are various.  The negative *si* is used only with relative verbs (those where slot IV is filled):  hence *si* and *ha* are mutually exclusive.  Many of the tense-aspects either do not occur or are expressed by different formatives when I or IV are occupied.

The subject concords we have already seen in operation. They are obligatory, except with the infinitive (taking a *ku* in slot III) and a 'general' tense with a III-prefix *hu*. The absence of subject concords with *ku* is presumably a consequence of the subjects having been deleted, but the absence with *hu* is unexplained.  In Swahili, as in many languages (see Kuno 1971), the locative in a sentence with an indefinite underlying subject becomes the subject, expelling the original subject to a position after the verb.

The advancement of locative to subject manifests itself in Swahili with unusual clarity, because in such sentences the subject slot takes the locative concord appropriate to the locative notion intended, and the locative appears in front of the verb in characteristic subject position. This is true even when the locative is a prepositional phrase in such prepositions as *katika* 'in.'

Thus we have examples such as the following of (159). To keep the interlinear glosses manageable I adopt the following abbreviations: SG, singular class prefix; PL, plural class prefix; SB, subject concord; OB object concord; REL, relative kihusiano.

(159) a. Mwitu-ni   m-me-lala    wa-nyama.
       forest-LOC SB-PERF-sleep PL-animal
       'In the forest sleep animals.'

     b. Wanyama wamelala     mwituni.
       animals SB:PERF:sleep in the forest
       'The animals sleep in the forest.'

     c. Ki-banda-ni m-me-lala    wa-dudu.
       SG-shed-LOC SB-PERF-sleep PL-insect
       'In the shed sleep insects.'

     d. Kule mji-ni   ku-me-kufa  wa-tu.
       there town-LOC SB-PERF-die PL-person
       'In the town over there people have died.'

     e. Hapa pa-me-kufa  simba.
       here SB-PERF-die lion
       'Here has died a lion.'

     f. Katika sanduku m-me-lala    m-dudu.
       in     box     SB-PERF-sleep SG-insect
       'In the box is sleeping an insect.'

(with stative verbs such as *lala* 'sleep', the perfect aspect marker *me* is used to express the present). This gives us evidence that these locatives are all surface NP. In particular, PP such as those with *katika*, where there is evidence that the whole phrase is an NP, may be contrasted with PP in *kwa* and *na* where there is no such evidence.

Unlike the subject prefix, the object prefix is optional. There appears to be a relation between humanness and copyability; human direct objects are most desirous of being copied, while inanimate objects are least. Nonetheless, they all can be copied.   Below are examples:

(160)   a.  Ni-li-mw-ona    (mtoto).
            I-PAST-him-saw  (child)
            'I saw him (the child).'

        b.  Ni-li-ki-ona  ki-tabu.
            I-PAST-OB-saw SG-book
            'I saw the book.'

Swahili has an almost always obligatory Dative-movement
rule which takes indirect objects (which occasionally appear
unmoved as prepositional phrases with the preposition *kwa*)
and places them directly in front of the direct object and
after the main verb. Hence the moved indirect object acquires the syntactic position of a direct object.   At the
same time, the verb gets its object concord from the moved
indirect object rather than from the direct object:

(161)   a.  Ni-li-m-pe       m-toto   ki-tabu.
            I-PAST-him-give SG-child SG-book
            'I gave the child the book.'

        b.  *Nilikipe kitabu mtoto.

            (O.K. with the nonsensical reading 'I gave the child to
            the book.')

        c.  *Nilikipe mtoto kitabu.

This shows that the verb is agreeing with the first NP in
the verb.

    We have seen that there are rules copying subject and
object clitic forms onto the verb.   David Perlmutter has
observed that when clitics are formed and moved, there are
only two places they can go:   to the verb, as they do in
Swahili, or to second position in the sentence, as they do
in Warlpiri (of course, this applies only to clitics formed
from major constituents of the sentence:   clitics formed
within an NP, such as copies of the possessor of that NP,
will move the head N, and likewise in PP).   This suggests
that a grammatical description of clitics in a language will
consist of two components:   one which says where, when formed, they will go.   The other component describes the conditions under which they are formed in the first place. In
Swahili, the grammar will contain a statement to the effect

that clitics go to the verb, and it will furthermore contain the two statements that subject clitics are generated
obligatorily and that object clitics are generated optionally.  The movement statement will then cause them to be
swept to the verb.  Once they get there, they will be ordered by a Surface Structure Constraint in the manner of
Perlmutter (1971).

1.2.1.2.3 *Relative Verbs:*  Swahili relative clauses fall
into two classes:  those with a relative kihusiano in slot
IV of the verb of $S_{rel}$, and those with the kihusiano attached to a particle *amba* appearing at the front of the clause.
Since the restrictions on the former construction reveal
the nature of the latter and the reasons for its existence,
I shall discuss the former first.

When a relative kihusiano appears in slot IV, the number
of possible tense-aspect distinctions becomes greatly reduced.  If the verb is negative, negation must be expressed
by a prefix *si* appearing in slot III, the tense-aspect slot,
and all tense-aspect distinctions become neutralized.  There
is also a generic relative, in which slot III is empty and
slot IV hops around to the end of the verb, slots II and V
remaining in their old positions, and there are in addition
progressive *(na)* past *(li)* and future *(taka)* tenses, to the
exclusion of all others.

The question now arises:  what fills slot IV and how
does it get there?  Slot IV is filled with the kihusiano of
$NP_{rel}$.  However, in order for the kihusiano to get there,
and hence for a relative verb to be possible, $NP_{rel}$ must
bear an appropriate syntactic relation to $S_{rel}$.

I will examine what happens when $NP_{rel}$ bears various
syntactic relations to $S_{rel}$.  When $NP_{rel}$ is the subject,
both the relative kihusiano and the subject concord appear
on the verb.  We have therefore examples such as the
following:

    (162)  a.  m-tu    a-li-ye-ki-soma        ki-tabu hiki
               SG-man  SB-PAST-REL-OB-read     SG-book this
               'a man who read this book'

b. m-tu    a-si-ye-soma
   SG-man SB-NEG-REL-read
   'a man who does not read'

c. Mimi n-a-sema    ni-taka-ye-kuwa
   I    SB-PRES-sat SB-FUT-REL-be
   Sultani wenu
   Sutan   your
   'I say it, who will be your Sultan.'

From these examples, you can discern various things about
the rule generating relative vihusiano. First of all, it
is a rule distinct from the one generating subject concords.
In these examples, both rules apply. Secondly, all the
rule has to do is specify that a relative vihusiano is
created. I propose that this creation itself proceeds in
two steps. First, there is a specification that $NP_{rel}$ is
specially marked, and then there is a specification that it
produces a clitic. The creation of the relative clitic is
quite independent of the creation of the subject clitic,
and subsequent to these processes, pronoun deletion dis-
poses of $NP_{rel}$. The vihusiano, as well as all the other
clitics, actually get to the verb by a rule which merely
moves clitics to the verb. This rule appears to apply at
various stages of the derivation: for example, after subject clitic formation, and also after kihuisiano formation.
Note from (162c) that even when $NP_{rel}$ is first person, one
gets the 3rd person kihusiano. I don't know why this is
the case.

   If $NP_{rel}$ is object, its kihusiano also appears on the
verb, and the object concord may or may not appear:

(163) a. mtu u-na-ye-m-saidia
         man you-PROG-REL-him-assist
         'the person you are assisting'

      b. ki-tabu a-ki-taka-cho Hamisi
         SG-book he-OB-want-REL Hamisi
         'the book which Hamisi wants'

      c. kitabu atakacho Hamisi
         'the book which Hamisi wants'

These sentences illustrate another rule which has the effect
of moving the relative verb to the front of the relative
clause, instead of leaving it behind the subject where it

normally would appear in a main clause.

If $NP_{rel}$ is the direct object of a verb that has an indirect object in the construction where the indirect object is a naked NP preceding the direct object, then its kihusiano still appears on the verb, even though an object concord for $NP_{rel}$ is in this case quite impossible:

```
(164)   barua  ni-taka-yo-mw-andikia
        letter I-FUT-REL-him-write
        'the letter which I shall write to him'
```

This last example illustrates quite clearly the independence of relative kihusiano creation from subject and object concord creation.

Relative vihusiano are found attached to the verb with two further types of $NP_{rel}$; $NP_{rel}$ which are objects of the prepositions *kwa* and *na* (*kwa* rather rarely), and $NP_{rel}$ which are adverbial modifiers of place, time and manner. Examples of these phenomena are given below:

```
(165)   a.  ma-embe   ni-li-yo-kuwa na-yo
            PL-mango  I-PAST-REL-be with-them
            'the mangoes which I was with,' meaning
            'the mangoes which I had'

        b.  fimbo u-li-yo-pig-wa            na-yo
            stick you-PAST-REL-hit-PASSIVE with-it
            'the stick that you were hit with'

        c.  rafiki   ni-li-o-sema     na-o
            friends  I-PAST-REL-talk with-them
            'my friends who I was talking with'

        d.  a-ta-weze       ku-salimika na   ile ibu
            he-FUT-be able INF-escape   from the stigma
            wa-li-yo-m-tia                chapa kwa-yo wa-zee   wake
            they-PAST-REL-him-put brand with-it PL-elder his
            'Will he be able to escape the stigma with which his
            parents have branded him?'
```

While $NP_{rel}$ is a locative in $S_{rel}$, $NP_{hd}$ may function either as a subject or object or an adverbial in the main clause:

```
(166)   a.  tu-me-pa-ona            a-li-po-pigana
            we-PERF-OB-see there he-PAST-REL-fight
                                          (loc)
                na    simba
                with  lion
            'We have seen the spot where he fought with the lion.'
```

b.  hamna         kitanda chumba-ni a-na-mo-lala
    there is not bed     room-LOC he-PROG-REL-sleep
    'There is not a bed in the room in which he is
    sleeping.'

When NP$_{rel}$ is temporal, locative vihusiano, notably *po*, are
used.  When it is a manner adverbial, the special kihusiano
*vyo* is used:

(167)  a.  a-li-po-sema,   waṭu   wakakimbia
           he-PAST-REL-say people fled
                (temp)
           'When he spoke, the people all fled.'

       b.  i-li-tuka        jinsi u-li-vyo-eleza
           SB-PAST-happen manner you-PAST-REL-explain
                                  (manner)
           'It happened in the manner that you have
           explained.'

We can observe that all of the usages of the relative
verb have it in common that NP$_{rel}$ is dominated by S$_{rel}$ without there being an NP dominating NP$_{rel}$ and dominated by
S$_{rel}$.  In fact, if NP$_{rel}$ is the object of the complement of
a verb, the possessor of something, or the object of a substantial preposition such as *katika* 'in' (remember that
*katika* phrases show agreement evidence of being NP), the
relative verb cannot be used.  Relative marking in Swahili
thus appears to obey the original A-over-A constraint.

In order to express a relative clause in which NP$_{rel}$ is
buried inside another NP, it is necessary to use the *amba*-
construction, which I discuss in the next section.  Note
that this account of the constraint depends crucially on
*kwa* and *na* phrases not being NP at the time NP$_{rel}$ applies
(presumably deep structure).

1.2.1.2.4 *Amba*:  Relative clauses in which NP$_{rel}$ is buried
under NP can be expressed by the *amba* construction, and
relative clauses in which NP$_{rel}$ is not so buried can be too.
Hence the *amba* construction can always be used in place of
a relative verb.  In this construction the kihusiano of
NP$_{rel}$ appears attached to the word *amba*, which begins the
clause, and the verb is a normal verb with all the tense,
mood and negation possibilities of a main clause verb.  Some
examples of the *amba* construction are as follows:

(168) a. Wi-tu     amba-vyo h-u-ta-vi-taka      kesho
          PL-thing *amba*-REL NEG-you-FUT-them-want tomorrow
          vi-weke   sandukuni.
          them-put into the box
          'Put the things which you will not want tomorrow into
          the box.'

     b. Yale       amba-yo kwa-yo a-li-wa-dangaya
          those PL-word *amba*-REL by-them he-PAST-them-deceived
          wenziwe        ha-ya-sahaulik-i.
          companions-his NEG-they-be forgotten-NEG
          'Those statements by which he deceived his companions
          will not be forgotten.'

     c. Wa-na-weze       ku-chukua ma-sanduku ma-kubwa,
          they-PROG-be able to-carry PL-box      PL-big
          amba-yo sisi watu    wawili au watatu
          *amba*-REL us   people two    or three
          ha-tu-wez-i       ku-ya-inua.
          NEG-we-be able-NEG INF-them-lift
                                    (*not* REL)
          'They are able to carry huge boxes which two or even
          three of us could not lift.'

     d. Walifika    katika bustani amba-yo  ndani    yake
          they arrived in    garden  *amba*-REL interior its
          mna       ma-ua    ya kila rangi.
          were in PL-flower of every color
          'They came to a garden in which were flowers of every
          color.'

     e. Ile nyumba amba-yo  paa  lake li-me-ungua.
          the house  amba-REL roof its  SB-PERF-scorched
          'The house, the roof of which was scorched'

     f. Yule jumbe     amba-ye tu-li-zugumza      habari zake.
          the  messenger *amba*-REL we-PAST-converse news   his
          'the messenger about whom we were conversing'

It is clear from the above examples that $NP_{rel}$ in the clause
following *amba* is being treated exactly as an ordinary pronoun. The question then is how does *amba* preserve $NP_{rel}$
from marking, and why does it allow $NP_{rel}$ to appear within
NP and complement S?

The *amba* construction is rather new:  until around the
turn of the century, structures that one must use *amba* to
relativize were unrelativizable in Swahili.  Furthermore,
*amba* is the stem of a verb meaning 'to speak.'  Although
*amba* alone has dropped out of usage, one of its voice-deriva-
tives, *ambia* 'to speak to' is still widely used. D. Permutter
tells me that in languages where there are strong restrictions

on what may be relativized, a very common way of evading
these restrictions is to say such things as 'the book of
which I say that Mary believes John wrote it.' Note that
in this sentence, $NP_{rel}$ is in the topmost clause, and it
has a coreferent embedded inside a *believe*-clause, which in
a language like Swahili would be an impossible context to
relativize out of directly. I therefore propose that *amba*
is in fact a highly defective, semantically empty verb,
which takes two arguments: $NP_{rel}$, and the S which expresses
the content of the relative clause. This would allow us to
keep a simple restriction on $NP_{rel}$ marking in Swahili, with
the *amba* construction being a frozen form of a construction
designed to evade the effects of the constraint. I believe
that this hypothesis is attractive, and its further verifi-
cation should prove an interesting task.

There are two further sets of facts which the hypothesis
must come to grips with, although I am not sure of their
significance. First, there are sentences in which a relative kihusiano appears both on *amba* and on the verb:

(169)  a. mimi amba-ye  ni-taka-ye watoto   si-wa-pata
          I    *amba*-REL I-want-REL children NEG:I-them-receive
          'I who want children do not get them.'

       b. mahali amba-po  i-li-po-fungiliwa       bandera ya
          place  *amba*-REL SB-PAST-REL-be unfurled flag     of
            Kiingereza
            England
          'a place where the British flat had been unfurled'

I suspect that this may have something to do with the 'double relativization' in English that we find in such sentences as 'The man who they tortured by burning holes in with
cigarettes was not pleased.' For some reason, both $NP_{rel}$
and its coreferent in the complement of *amba* acquire the
$NP_{rel}$ mark, and both are treated as usual by the cliticization rule applying to NP bearing this mark.

Secondly, there are certain dialects in which not only
does *amba* get the kihusiano of $NP_{rel}$ suffixed to it, but it
also gets the subject concord of $NP_{rel}$ prefixed to it, just
as if $NP_{rel}$ were its near-surface subject. Hence in the
KiVumba dialect of the southern Kenya coast (East African

100

Swahili Committee, 1956-1958) we have sentences such as the following:

(170) a. Jambo l-amba-lo    l-a-ni-dhuru     ndi-lo hili.
         thing SB-*amba*-REL SB-PRES-me-hurts is-it  this
         'The thing that hurts me is this.'

      b. Wewe w-amba-e    ku-na-n-amba     ni mwivi mbona
         you  SB-*amba*-REL you-PERF-me-say I  thief why
          k'-u-vi-ono        vy-amba-vyo si-kw-achii.
          you-NEG-them-see SB-amba-REL I-you-left
         'You who accuse me of being a thief, why did you not
          notice the things I left for you?'

A final fact is that in this dialect, as well as in the standard language, the *amba* may be followed by *kwamba*, a complementizer frequently used to introduce indirect discourse.  Hence we have these examples:

(171) a. Ni-me-sikia kwamba mwitu u-ki-washwa      moto,
         I-PERF-heard that   forest SB-if-is put to fire
         u-ta-ungua  wote.
         SB-FUT-burn all
         'I have heard that if fire is put to the forest it
          will burn away completely.'

      b. Watu    amba-o    kwamba wa tayari.
         people amba-REL  that    SB ready
         'people who are ready'

These examples suggest that the surface structure of the *amba*-relative is roughly like (172):

(172)

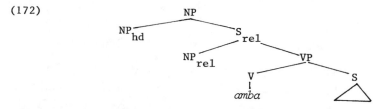

The apparent peculiarities of the *amba*-relative clauses may thus have a reasonable explanation, with the complexities in NP$_{rel}$ marking being consequences of its interaction with other constructions.  This concludes my discussion of Swahili.

1.2.1.3  *General Remarks on NP$_{rel}$ Marking:*  We may observe that there is also NP$_{rel}$ marking not associated with movement in the Indic languages discussed earlier:  Sanskrit, Hindi and Marathi, as well as in Mabuiag.  Although relative pronouns often wind up at the front of the sentence in the Indic languages, their propensity for scrambling makes it difficult to tell whether $NP_{rel}$ is scrambled to the front, or gets there by a special optional rule.

What is the mechanism for $NP_{rel}$ marking?  We could have the markers be generated in the base, or transformationally. There is little solid ground to determine the choice.  In Section 2.3 I will describe a proposal for performing the marking in the base.

One will observe that the vast majority of languages that have marking of $NP_{rel}$ in an embedded relative con-struction have it in a post-relative structure.  I know of only two languages that have it in pre-relatives, the closely related Northwest Caucasian languages Abkhaz and Abaza.  In these languages, $NP_{rel}$ is deleted by ordinary pronominalization processes, but regular rules which put agreement markers on constituents to which the NP bears certain grammatical relations (subject, object, possessor, etc.) put the markers in a special form when the NP is $NP_{rel}$.  These phenomena are described in Anderson, (in pre-paration).

We may finally observe that the paucal relative of English (section 1.1.2.2) provides an example of $NP_{rel}$ marking in an internal head relative clause.  We thus see that $NP_{rel}$ may be marked in all the varieties of relative clause structure that we have discerned.

1.2.2 *Deletion of $NP_{rel}$*:  In many languages, $NP_{rel}$ merely disappears.  There is a fundamental question of mechanism to which we have no answer:  does the disappearance come about by a *bona fide* deletion transformation, or is there instead generation of a phonologically null element in the deep structure position of $NP_{rel}$?  Lacking an answer to this question, I shall speak of $NP_{rel}$ Deletion knowing that the term 'Deletion' is perhaps merely suggestive.

Perlmutter (1972) suggested a test for distinguishing languages with deletion of $NP_{rel}$ from languages in which there was free deletion of anaphoric pronouns, including $NP_{rel}$.  He proposed that the former, but not the latter,

languages obeyed island constraints. Recent work by Keenan
(1972) calls this into doubt. Keenan observes that many
languages in which $NP_{rel}$ is represented by a pronoun rather
than being deleted obey island-like constraints on where
$NP_{rel}$ may be found.

For these reasons, I will accept as true $NP_{rel}$ Deletion
languages only languages in which there are $NP_{rel}$ that disappear that could not be removed by free pronoun deletion.
I will consider two such languages: Turkish, where the
deletion happens in a pre-relative clause, and Modern Greek,
in which it takes place in a post-relative.

1.2.2.1 *Turkish*: In section 1.1.1.2.2, I said that Turkish
had deletion of $NP_{rel}$, but I did not demonstrate it. This
I will now proceed to do.

In Turkish, unstressed subject and possessor pronouns
are regularly dropped. Hence one gets examples like (173):

    (173)  a.  Gel-di.
               come-PAST
               'He came.'

          b.  Hasan baba-sı-nı     gördü.
              Hasan father-his-ACC saw
              'Hasan saw his father.'  (Hasan's or someone else's)

          c.  Hasan Orhan-ını baba-sı-nı     gördü.
              Hasan Orhan-GEN father-his-ACC saw
              'Hasan saw Orhan's father.'

In (173a) the subject pronoun has disappeared. In (173b)
the genitive pronoun with which the agreement suffix -*sı* is
agreeing has vanished. In (173c) we see a sentence with
full NP in the place of these missing ingredients.

Though subject and genitive pronouns vanish, object
pronouns do not. Hence we have these sentences:

    (174)  Hasan, Fatma-nın *(o-nu)   öl-dür-eceğ-i-ni     düşünüyor.
           Hasan Fatma-GEN (he-ACC) die-CAUSE-FUT-her-ACC thinks
           'Hasan$_i$ thinks that Fatma will kill him$_{i,j}$.'

We see that the object pronoun of (174) is not freely deletable. But when $NP_{rel}$ is a direct object, it always disappears:

(175)  Orhan-ın  (*o-nu)  gör-düg-ü   adam  çıktı.
       Orhan-GEN  (he-ACC)  see-NOM-his man  left
       'The man who Orhan saw left.'

This deletion of the pronoun shows that there is in fact a
rule of NP$_{rel}$ deletion at work.

We can see an interesting contrast between Turkish and
English.  Both English and Turkish have free relatives.
The Turkish free relative looks exactly like a pre-relative,
but has no head.  Hence we have (176):

(176)  Hasan-ın  al-dığ-ı-nı      gördüm.
       Hasan-GEN  buy-NOM-his-ACC I saw
       'I saw what Hasan bought.'

In English, however, we must form the free relative with a
relative pronoun:  we cannot use the *that*-relative or the
*that*-less relative construction.  It would appear then that
we would need two kinds of NP$_{rel}$ deletion:  one kind sensitive to the presence of a head, and the other kind not.
There is, however, a possible escape from this conclusion.

We can paraphrase (176) with (177), which is identical
in structure, except that the relative clause is a pre-
relative on the head *şey* 'thing.':

(177)  Hasanın aldığı şeyi gördüm.

We could claim that (176) was derived from (177) by a rule
of *şey*-deletion.  An immediate objection to this proposal
is that one should not delete lexical items.  This may be
countered by proposing that *şey* is a 'pronominal N':  a
noun head that is really a pronoun, like 'place,' 'time,'
and 'thing' in English.  Since pronouns are members of a
closed category, their deletion is not in principle as
objectionable as deletion of real lexical items.  See
Andrews (1974) for discussion.  I add as a cautionary note,
however, that Navajo, which offers a free relative construction that cannot be analysed as a headed relative clause,
does not need to have a rule of NP$_{rel}$ deletion.  This
potential source of testimony as to whether there is NP$_{rel}$
deletion in underlying headless relative clauses is not in
fact available.

1.2.2.2 *Modern Greek:*  Modern Greek has two relative clause
constructions.  One, characteristic of the literary (Kath-
arevousa) language, has a relative pronoun *o opíos* (taking
various inflectional forms) that is preposed to the front
of the relative clause.  *o opíos* is distinct from the interrogative pronouns *piós* 'who?' *ti* 'what?'.  The other construction, characteristic of the colloquial (Demotic) language, has a relative complementizer *pu*.  $NP_{rel}$ is deleted
or retained as a pronoun.  I shall here investigate the
properties of the *pu*-relative.

Modern Greek is an SVO language with scrambling, prepositions, preceding complementizers and conjunctions, and
post-relative clauses.  There are three cases on NP:  nominative, genitive and accusative.  Pronouns come in both
clitic and nonclitic forms.  Verbs are inflected for the
person and number of their subjects, and there are no subject clitics, nonemphatic subjects being simply deleted.
Nonemphatic direct and indirect objects appear as clitic
pronouns on the verb, the direct object clitics being
accusative, the indirect objects genitive.  Full NP indirect
objects do not appear in the genitive, but rather as objects
of the preposition *se*, of which we will have more to say in
the sequel.  In addition to case, nouns and their depen-
dents are inflected for number (sg/pl) and gender (masc/fem/
neut).  These markings will not be noted in the glosses.

We can see from the following examples that ordinary
anaphoric object pronoun clitics are not deleted freely:

(178)  a.  O        leonídhas     vríke ton      kósta      ke
           The:NOM Leonidas:NOM found the:ACC Costa:ACC and
           i       maríka    *(ton)   skótose.
           the:NOM Maria:NOM him:ACC killed
           'Leonidas found Costa and Maria killed him.'

       b.  O        leonídhas     nomízi oti i       maríka
           the:NOM Leonidas:NOM thinks that the:NOM Maria:NOM
           tha *(ton)     skotosi.
           FUT  him:ACC kill
           'Leonidhas thinks that Maria will kill him.'

However an $NP_{rel}$ object of a verb must be deleted:

(179)  O        ándras  pu  (*ton)  ídha íne o        leonídhas.
       the:NOM man:NOM REL   him:ACC I    is the:NOM Leonidas:NOM
       'The man who I saw is Leonidas."

Indirect object and possessive clitics, on the other hand,
must be left behind in clitic form as 'returning pronouns':

(180) a.  i  yinéka pu *(tis)  édhosa to vivlío
          the woman REL she:GEN I gave the book
          'the woman who I gave the book to'

      b.  i  yinéka pu éklepsa to vivlío *(tis)
          the woman REL I stole the book  she:GEN
          'the woman whose book I stole'

It is worth noting that in poetry, accusative $NP_{rel}$ may be
left behind, as, for example, in the following two lines of
Seferis:

(181)  páno s-to  dzámi afto pu  to xtipá   i  vroxi apo ton
       upon at-the window this REL it strikes the rain  from the
       ékso    kósmo
       outside world
       'upon this window struck by the rain/from the outside
       world' (Mythistorema 6, Keeley and Sherrard (1969)).

We may observe that it is the genitive clitics that are
left behind, and the accusatives (and presumably the nom-
inatives) that are deleted.

There is a constraint on relativization that $NP_{rel}$ must
either be deleted or appear as a clitic pronoun. Full NP
or nonclitic pronominal NP are ungrammatical. This fact,
together with some features of the system of prepositions,
leads to there being an entertainingly unsayable class of
sentences in Modern Greek. To exhibit them, we must investigate the syntax of prepositional phrases.

There are two kinds of prepositions in Modern Greek.
There are first the simple prepositions, which take accusative NP objects. Some of these are se 'to, at, on'; me
'with'; apo 'from'; ya 'for'; xorís, dhíxos 'without'.
The simple prepositions take their objects in the accusative
case. Hence we have s-to trapézi 'on the table', me tin
kopéla 'with the girl', apo to xorió 'from the village'.
Nonclitic pronouns are treated exactly like ordinary NP:
s' aftón 'to him'. But there is a constraint that the
object cannot be a clitic: *ston, *stou, *me ton, *me tu,

etc. Since *se*, *me*, and *apo* are clearly proclitics, we might explain the phenomenon by proposing a restriction that a clitic cannot take a clitic as head. But since the status of the other simple prepositions is not clear to me, I cannot rely on this explanation for the constraint.

Then there are the adverbial prepositions, which are much more numerous than are the simple ones. These include *mazí* 'with', *kondá* 'near', and *káto* 'under'. They take as objects not NP, but prepositional phrases in the three simple prepositions *se*, *me* and *apo* ('at/to', 'with' and 'from'). We hence find *mazí me to korítsi* 'with the girl', *kondá sto spiti* 'near the house', and *káto apo to trapézi* 'under the table', *mazí me aftín* 'with her'. There is also a construction in which the adverbial prepositions take a clitic pronominal object. In place of the simple prepositional phrase, one merely puts a genitive clitic: *mazí tis* 'with her', *kondá tu* 'near him', *káto tu* 'under it, him'. It is thus the case that clitic objects can only appear with the adverbial prepositions. It is also worth noting that the adverbial prepositions, but not the simple ones, can take 'predeterminer modification' as described by Bresnan (1973) and extended to English prepositional phrases by Jackendoff (1973): *pio pera apo ta vuná* 'further beyond the mountains'. This fact, as well as the cliticization phenomena, suggests that the adverbial prepositions have a significant featural relationship to the major categories. There is no such evidence for the simple prepositions.

Now let us consider relativization. If $NP_{rel}$ is the object of an adverbial preposition, $NP_{rel}$ is represented by a genitive clitic on the preposition, and there is no problem:

(182)  i    kopéla pu  káthisa kondá tis
       the girl   REL I sat    near  her:GEN
       "the girl I sat near"

If, however, $NP_{rel}$ is the object of a simple preposition, the *pu* construction simply can't be used:

(183) *i   kopéla pu  mílisa  me    tin
       the girl   REL I spoke with   aftin
                                     her

We are forced to use the relative pronoun *o opios*:

(184)  i   kopéla me   tin   opían mílisa
       the girl  with whom      I spoke
       "the girl with whom I spoke"

The morphologically sensitive reader will perhaps have
noted that *o opíos* is of the form *Definite Article + opíos*,
a form parallel in its make-up to Fr. *lequel*, It. *il quale*
and the archaic English *the which*. It is surely not acci-
dental or a consequence of borrowing that so many relative
pronouns are of this form.

On the basis of Modern Greek, we make an observation
that is of interest in the formalization of relativization
rules. There are two morphological entities that may
serve as $NP_{rel}$: a clitic pronoun, and the relative pronoun
*o opíos*. The latter, but not the former, preposes. This
shows that the rule is being conditioned not merely by the
fact that a certain NP is $NP_{rel}$, but by the presence of an
actual formative.

1.2.3 *Movement of $NP_{rel}$*: Movement of $NP_{rel}$ is sufficiently
familiar to need little discussion here. I wish, however,
to make certain observations.

It is generally held that the head of a relative clause
is part of the environment for fronting in a relative
clause. If English headless relatives are derived from
underlyingly headless structures, then this position is
untenable. Rather, the conditioning factor would presumably be the 'R' that I propose appears as the complementizer of relative clauses.

Recent work by Chomsky (1973) is compatible with this
claim. Chomsky writes *wh* Movement as follows (Chomsky
1973 ex. 199b):

(185) *wh* Movement: in the structure
      $[_S[_{COMP} X_1, X_2, X_3, \pm WH], X_5, wh, X_7]$
      the sixth term fills the position of $X_2$ and
      is replaced by PRO.

+WH is Q; -WH is R and also the *that* in ordinary complements. Hence (185) is *wh* Movement in both questions and

relative clauses. The *'wh'* in term 6 is not the formative *wh*, but a feature attached to the constituent that actually moves. Hence, in *to whom did you talk?*, the *wh* is attached to the prepositional phrase *to whom*.

This treatment avoids a difficulty which would otherwise appear in Chomsky's theory of *wh* Movement. Chomsky proposes that *wh* Movement removes a *wh* word from an embedded S by moving it on each cycle to the COMP of the $\bar{S}$ being cycled on. Hence one gets *who does Bill think Mary likes* by way of the intermediate stage *Bill thinks who Mary likes*. Since *wh* Movement may either extract an NP from within a PP or else move the whole PP, we have a problem in explaining the ungrammaticality of *who does Bill think to Mary gave a record*. By saying that in the underlying structure of *to whom does Bill think Mary gave a record*, the feature *wh* is attached to the PP, we explain why the entire PP must again move when we reapply (185) to the intermediate structure *Bill thinks to whom Mary gave a book*.

This formalization also accomplishes the desirable effect of eliminating the 'Pied Piping Convention' of Ross (1967). In Pied Piping, the *wh* movement transformation mentions a *wh*-marked term, and the rule actually moves another. An attempt to build this into a theory of rule application would involve substantial complications. Under Chomsky's treatment, the terms mentioned in the structural description are those used in the structural change.

Recent work by Bresnan, some of which is presented in Bresnan (1974b), promises to provide an alternative to Chomsky's account in which both the Pied Piping Convention and the abstract *wh* are eliminated.

I will close by pointing out that preposing of NP$_{rel}$ is a minority strategy: it is quite common in Indo-European, but rather rare otherwise. I might also add that I have found no counterexamples to the claim of Bresnan (1970) that *wh* words in relative clauses and questions move across variables to the left, but not to the right.

1.3 *The Extraction Analysis:* I will here discuss a variety of languages in which there exist phenomena that suggest the

correctness of the proposal that the heads of embedded
relative clauses with heads are extracted from within them.
I do not believe that these descriptions contain knockdown
arguments for the proposals, but the situations described
are such that both friends and foes of this analysis should
investigate carefully.

1.3.1 *Japanese:* In many languages, we observe a restriction that when the embedded relative clause has a head,
$NP_{rel}$ must be pronominal. This is compatible with and
somewhat supportive of the extraction analysis. On the
other hand, it would appear that if $NP_{rel}$ and $NP_{hd}$ could be
full NP with different head NP, the extraction analysis
would be completely disconfirmed.

At first blush this is the situation obtaining in
Japanese. In section 1.1.1.2.2 I observed the grammaticality of the following:

> (186)  watakusi ga   sono hito   no namae    wasurete simatta
>        I        SUBJ that person GEN name OBJ have forgotten
>        okyaku-san
>        guest
>     "a guest whose name I have forgotten"

Martin (1972) describes a similar construction which
appears in certain dialects of English: "They are the guys
who Bill says the bastards stole your car!" This construction is highly marginal, many speakers rejecting it
out of hand. The position of $NP_{rel}$ is occupied by an
epithet, and the entire construction has a distinctly
pejorative tone. (186), on the other hand, is a perfectly
ordinary noun phrase of Japanese. I suspect, then, that
Martin's examples are derived by some sort of non-trans-
formational deformation of syntactic structures: amalga-
matory insertion of an epithet into an empty position
created by the preposing of *who*. The process is perhaps a
syntactic counterpart to the phonetic and morphological
deformations described in Nootka by Sapir (1963).

(186), on the other hand, appears to be a *bona fide*
product of Japanese syntax, and to destroy any hope for
an extraction analysis of Japanese relative clauses. There
are, however, considerations which potentially reverse

the import of (186).

Kuno (1973) has proposed that $NP_{rel}$ in Japanese is always the theme of $NP_{rel}$: the theme being the preposed NP followed by *wa* that was mentioned in 1.1.1.2.2. The theme needn't have a co-referent in the clause. If there is a coreferent, however, it is most usual for it to be deleted. But under certain circumstances it needn't be, and may surface as a full NP with head N distinct from that of the theme. I refer the reader to Kuno (1973) and McCawley (1972) for discussion. We have thus (187), in which the theme has no coreferent, and (188), in which the coreferent of the theme is a full NP distinct from the theme:

(187)  Sakana wa    tai        ga   ii
       fish   THEME red-snapper SUBJ good-is
       "Speaking of fish, red snapper is the best."

(188)  Ano  okyaku-san wa    watakusi ga   sono hito   no
       that guest       THEME I        SUBJ that person GEN
         namae o   wasurete simatta.
         name  OBJ have forgotten
       "Speaking of that guest, I have forgotten his name."

There is, however, the requirement, common to all anaphora, that the coreferent be a more general noun phrase than the initial theme. Hence (189) is ungrammatical:

(189) *Ano  hito    wa    watakusi ga   sono okyaku-san no   namae
       that person THEME I        SUBJ that guest        GEN name
        o    wasurete simatta.
        OBJ have forgotten.

With this in mind, we may reconsider (186).

It is required that there be no theme on the surface in relative clauses. Hence (190) are ungrammatical noun phrases:

(190)  a.  *Sono okyakusan wa watakusi ga sono hito no
             namae o wasurete simatta  okyakusan

       b.  *Sono hito wa watakusi ga sono hito no
             namae o wasurete simatta okyakus-san.

This theme must then obligatorily disappear.

Fiengo (1974) has pointed out the suspicious nature of positing elements which are 'positive absolute exceptions' to deletion: elements that are obligatorily identical to

some other element and obligatorily delete under identity
with it.  We have two alternatives to postulating that the
vanishing theme of the relative clause is obligatorily
identical to the head and obligatorily deleted due to
identity with it.  We can suppose that the theme is moved
into head position, or we can suppose that it is underlying
a pronoun or a null element.  If we pick this latter alternative, we will be violating the generalization noted with
respect to *(189), that a theme must be less general than
its coreferent.  The former analysis avoids this problem,
as well as the problem of positing such obligatorily identical obligatorily deleting elements.

As the extraction hypothesis would predict, and as we
would expect anyway, the head of the relative clause must
be less general than any surviving coreferents within it.
Hence (191) is bad, just as is (189):

(191)  *Watakusi ga    sono okyakusan no   namae o
        I          SUBJ that guest     GEN name  OBJ
          wasurete simatta hito.
          have forgotten    person
        "the guest/person whose name I have forgotten"

Kuno's hypothesis removes (186) from the class of clear
counterexamples to the extraction anlysis, and may well
convert it into a strong argument for the proposal.  It
also eliminates a counterexample to the general claim that
when there is a head to an embedded relative clause, $NP_{rel}$
must delete or be pronominal.

1.3.2 *Micmac:*  This example was presented by Hale (1970).
It involves the category of obviation.  When there are two
third person NP in an S, the second becomes obviative.  This
is illustrated in the following:

(192)  a.  Tjĩmn elogoet.
           man   work
           "The man is working."

       b.  Ēpit nemiat-1   tjĩmno-1
           woman see-OBV.OB man-OBV
           "The woman sees the man."

But if the subject of a sentence (the first NP in it) is
$NP_{hd}$ of a relative clause in which $NP_{rel}$ is the object

(second NP in $S_{rel}$), then $NP_{hd}$ becomes obviative in accordance with the structure of the main clause:

(193)  Tjĩmno-1 tān ēpit nemiat-1   na
       man-OBV REL woman see-OBV.OB prt work-OBV.SUBJ
       "The man who the woman sees is working."

$NP_{hd}$ is thus here being assigned to a grammatical category on the basis of the status of $NP_{rel}$.

1.3.3 *Persian:* Persian is an SOV language, but it has prepositions preceding conjunctions, and following modifiers in NP. Relativization is reminiscent of that in Demotic Greek. The relative clause is a post-relative, with $NP_{rel}$ deleted if it is a subject or an object, otherwise left behind as a pronoun. There is, however, no clitic/nonclitic distinction.

There is a formative *e* (which I gloss MD for 'modifier'), which is attached to the head of any post-head modifier if that modifier is itself followed by a modifier. There is also a Specific Accusative marker *ra*, which I shall gloss as ACC. This marks direct objects that are specific. See Browne (1972) for discussion of the function of *ra*. *ra* follows the NP, and *e* is not inserted before it. Hence we have the following:

(194)  a.  ketab-e bozorg (ra)
           book-MD big    ACC
           "(the) big book"

       b.  ketab-e bozorg-e mæn (ra)
           book-MD big-MD   I   ACC
           "my big book"

Note that possession is rendered as in (194b) by placing the possessor NP after the head as if it were an adjective.

In the relative clause construction, the *e* does not appear. Instead, $NP_{hd}$ is followed by a formative *i* which may also be placed after an NP to render it indefinite. Hence:

(195)  a.  ketab-i (ra) ke didæm
           book-IND ACC REL I saw
           "the book I saw"

       b.  mærd-i ke be u  ketab didæm
           man-IND REL to him book I gave
           "the man I gave a book to"

But there is a strange twist in the use of *ra*. Normally, *ra* is obligatory in a specific object. But if one has an $NP_{hd}$ that is a direct object in the main clause, and $NP_{rel}$ is a subject in the relative, then *ra* is optional on $NP_{hd}$, and likewise, if $NP_{rel}$ is subject in the main clause and $NP_{rel}$ is object in the relative clause, then *ra* is also optional. Hence it appears that when an NP is modified by a relative clause one may look either at the role of $NP_{hd}$ in the matrix or of $NP_{rel}$ in the relative clause to determine the case-marking of $NP_{hd}$.

Some examples of this from Lambton (1953) are:

(194) a. An zæni (ra) ke diruz amæd didæm.
 that woman:IND (ACC) REL yesterday came I saw
 "I saw the woman who came yesterday."

b. Zæni (ra) ke didid injast.
 woman:IND (ACC) REL you saw is here
 "The woman you saw is here."

c. Ketab-i (ra) ke be mæn dadid gom šode æst.
 book-IND (ACC) REL to me you gave is lost

From these facts of case-marking, and from the appearance of the *i* (recall that $NP_{rel}$ in Crow internal head relative clauses have indefinite morphology), one might well be able to work up an argument that the heads of Persian relative clauses are extracted from within them.

Jeanne (1974) has proposed an analysis of Hopi relativization which makes crucial use of the inheritance by $NP_{hd}$ of the case of $NP_{rel}$ in a manner somewhat reminiscent of, although significantly different from, Persian.

Before leaving the subject, I will observe that the available evidence for the extraction analysis all involves cases where $NP_{rel}$ is not a relative pronoun, but is an ordinary pronoun or is deleted. Consider in English the contrast *the headway (that) we made* and **the headway which we made*. This is comforting in light of the fact that one of the major problems with the analysis is insuring that the *wh* formative on relative pronouns gets universally left behind during extraction.

114

## FOOTNOTES TO CHAPTER 1

1. Much of the research in this chapter was supported by grant OEC-O-70-4986(8234) from the Office of Education to Stephen Anderson at the Language Research Foundation. The contents of this chapter differ substantially both from the report to OEC co-authored with Anderson and also from various preliminary drafts of mine that have been informally circulated. Motu, Tagalog, French and Breton were omitted because Anderson wrote or revised the sketch, and Hopi, Welch and Dagbani were omitted for reasons of space and time. Japanese was added, and Navajo and Marathi were substantially expanded.

I am indebted to Ken Hale, Dave Perlmutter, Hu Matthews, Paul Kiparsky, Haj Ross, Mary Lou Walch and Roy Wright for commenting on earlier drafts of this chapter. I am also indebted to many people for helping me with particular languages. They are indicated in footnotes, in the text, and in the index of languages and sources that appears as an appendix to this chapter. I finally thank Stephen Anderson for getting me interested in the subject and supporting much of my work in it.

2. But note:

*Nobody got a pen, and he wrote a letter with it.
Nonrestrictive relatives seem to presuppose existence (example by Ross (personal communication)).

3. Sandy Chung has informed me that Churchward (1934), upon which this is based, is accurate for the modern language.

4. Robert Underhill taught me most of what I know about Eskimo.

5. I have been greatly assisted with Japanese by Susumu Kuno and Shosuke Haraguchi.

6. Wha-Chun Kim provided the information about Korean.

7. This analysis has now been published by Hale (1976).

8. Sharad Gupti was extremely generous of his time in teaching me enough about Marathi to write this section. S.D. Joshi volunteered the first referential multiple-headed relative clause I encountered. Kashi Wali has also

been quite helpful.

9.  Wayles Brown has given me advice on Persian.

APPENDIX TO CHAPTER 1 - INDEX OF LANGUAGES AND SOURCES

I give first the language, then the pages on which I discuss it, then references works on it, and finally those who have provided me with information about it.  Only languages receiving substantial discussions are mentioned.

Crow:  pp. 83-88; Lowie 1944; Dale Oldhorn, George Reed, Rose Chesarek.

English:  pp. 11-17, 48-53, 73-81.

Eskimo:  pp. 21-25; Kleinschmidt 1851, Schultz-Lorentzen 1945, Bergsland 1955; Robert Underhill.

Faroese:  pp. 20-21; Lockwood 1964.

Greek (Md.):  pp. 104-107; Dimitri Konstantinidi.

Hindi:  pp. 60-62; Donaldson 1971.

Hottentot:  pp. 36-38; Meinhof 1909.

Japanese:  pp. 26-30, 108-111; Kuno 1973, McCawley 1972; Susumu Kuno, Shosuke Haraguchi.

Mabuiag:  pp. 58-60; Klokeid 1970.

Marathi:  pp. 64-73; Southworth and Kavadi 1965; Sharad Gupte, Kashi Wali, S.D. Joshi.

Micmac:  pg. 111; Hale 1970;

Navajo:  pp. 40-47, 110-121; Platero 1974, Perkins 1974, Kaufman 1974, Platero and Hale 1974; Ken Hale, Paul Platero.

Persian:  pp. 112-113; Lambton 1953, Brown 1970; Wayles Brown.

Samoan:  pp. 18-20; Churchward 1934; Sandy Chung.

Sanskrit:  pp. 62-64; Wackernagel 1930.

Swahili:  pp. 88-100; Ashton 1944, Loogman 1965, East African Swahili Committee 1956-58.

Tibetan:  pp. 34-35; Lalou 1950.

Turkish:  pp. 30-34; Lewis 1953, 1967, Underhill 1972.

Warlpiri:  pp. 55-58; Hale 1970, 1971, 1974 class lectures, 1976.

2. *Comparative Clauses:* In this chapter, I will devote my attention to the comparative clause construction of English. I will follow the arrangement, and, to a large degree, the content, of the classic article on the subject by Bresnan (1973).[1] I will first consider the head to which comparative clauses are attached, and then the relation between the head and the clause.

In the treatment of the head, I will adopt (with minor revisions) the analysis proposed by Bresnan, and will extend it to a construction not considered by her, the indefinite comparative construction of such examples as *the more you study, the less you know.* My primary concern will be, however, with the metatheory in which the analysis is formulated. I shall formulate certain processes which Bresnan leaves vague, such as the rule of QP Raising, and, more significantly, will propose a system of conventions on rule application and constraints on structure which, given some rather strong assumptions, allow one to make a case that the analysis given is in fact the most highly valued one for the data considered, and that in several cases, the most highly valued analysis for subsets of the data predicts the remainder. This amounts to making the claim that Bresnan's analysis is internally justified within a linguistic theory with a significant degree of explanatory adequacy.

Bresnan supposed that comparative clauses were generated within the determiners of the quantifier phrases that they modify. Using multiple headed comparatives that are similar to the multiple headed relative clauses of the preceding chapter, I will show that such a source is untenable. I shall propose that comparative clauses are generated in underlying structure in the position that they occupy on the surface, and will explain the phenomena previously taken to support determiner generation of comparatives in terms of a theory of extra-constituent structure relations of the sort extensively used in the previous chapter. This time, however, I will take a far more formal approach to the material, providing a formalization of the

representation of the relations, and proposing a system of
language-universal conditions governing permissable assign-
ments of systems of relations to constituent structures.
These principles will also cover relative clauses as presented in the previous chapter, and will therefore constitute a unified theory of determiner complementation.

2.1 *The Head, Revisited:* I will here review the analysis
provided by Bresnan of the head constituent to which the
comparative clause is attached.  I shall assume Bresnan's
base rules, and recast the transformational part of her
analysis within a particular metatheory.  I shall make a
case that if the basic data from which language learning
proceeds is assumed to consist of a set of surface string-
deep structure pairs, then the transformational part of
the analysis is the most highly valued analysis provided by
the metatheory that is consistent with the data.  I will
furthermore attempt to support certain articles of the metatheory on the grounds that they lead to analyses being
selected by subsets of the total range of data which those
analyses explain.  The analysis will thus be argued to be
internally justified, and the metatheory to be explanator-
ily potent.

The assumption that the basic data from which language
learning takes place consists of surface string-deep structure pairings is unrealistically strong.  Nonetheless, I
believe that results attained by means of it may be valid
and interesting.  For it is likely that given a sufficiently restrictive theory of the semantic interpretation of
deep structure, there may be relatively few ways of con-
struing a string of words and phrases of known meaning
into a sentence with a coherent reading.

Consider, for example, the phrase *many too many marbles.*
Suppose we are ignorant of the syntax of the language, but
we know that *many* and *too many* are quantity expressions,
the latter signifying excessive amount, and that *marbles* is
a count noun.  Then one of the few ways of taking the phrase
semantically will be to take the first *many* as qualifying
*too many,* and *many too many* as qualifying *marbles.*  About

the only alternative I can think of is to take it as the predication *many is too many marbles*, or something like that. The context might well serve to eliminate many formally possible ways of semantically combining the elements of the string.

Given a sufficiently restrictive theory of semantic interpretation, this string could lead to a uniquely determined addition to the base component of the language being learned: namely, the addition of the rules that generate a deep structure that can be interpreted as having the formally possible and pragmatically plausible reading, and which can be related to the string by a minimal, in this case by a null, set of transformations.

These results, if valid, have an interesting implication for research directed at constraining linguistic theory. The greatest part of such work has been devoted to constraining the transformational component, the base being comparatively neglected. In the following pages, I will assume a transformational component that is quite unconstrained by current standards of work in the Extended Standard Theory. It seems to me likely that if a sufficiently restrictive theory of the base were found, one could show that the theory determined the analysis for the data without making the assumption that the data included the deep structures for the strings considered. Rather, one would suppose the data to include information on the semantic type of words and phrases in the strings. The implication is that work on constraining linguistic theory should be focussed not on the transformational component, but on the base.

2.1.1 *Basic Structures:* I shall begin by reviewing Bresnan's basic analysis of QP, AP and predicative NP. I shall be concerned with the material in her sections 1.1 - 1.4, omitting partitives.

Bresnan has no analysis for nodes of type V (V, VP, and perhaps S, etc.), and her analysis of N nodes was essentially limited to the predicative or adjectival NP found in predicate nominal and certain nonreferential positions (e.g.

*I have never seen as magnificent a coelacanth as this
specimen*), although she ventures an occasional diagram for
ordinary NP. I shall remain within these limitations.
Although she did not formally adopt an X-bar analysis, her
analysis was so given as to be easily translated into one.

In Chomsky's (1970) exposition of the X-bar notation,
he proposed that there was a small set of language-universal primitive categories including at least N, V, A and S,
which might themselves be composed of features. There are
then four diacritic features: 0, 1, 2 and Spec.

The following rule skeletons are then specified:

(1)  a.  $S \longrightarrow N^2 V^2$

b.  $X^2 \longrightarrow [Spec, X^1] X^1$

c.  $X^1 \longrightarrow X \ldots$

'...' is to be the material in the complement of the various
categories. $[Spec, X^1]$ is taken to comprise the system of
articles, possessives and demonstratives; $[Spec, V^1]$ the
auxiliary system; and $[Spec, A^1]$ is hypothesized to comprise the system of degree modification.

Chomsky's schema (1a) is irrelevant to her discussion;
the other two, however, she accepts, but makes certain
changes in the framework. She adopts a new category Q,
which contains the quantifiers, such as *few, more, enough,*
etc. Note that the Q are the linguistic quantity expressions, rather than the logical operators ∃ and ∀. I shall
thus take the category variables in the rules as ranging
over N, V and A, with A comprising both adjectives and
adverbs. It would be wrong to attribute to Bresnan the
positions that the basic category features are N, Q and A.
Rather, she should be taken as suggesting that the basic
feature system should be so constructed to deliver these
categories, presumably along with others.

Furthermore, she alters the interpretation of the Spec
nodes. For $[Spec, N^1]$, she preserves Chomsky's interpretation, especially in putting the indefinite article there,
and also a null article that she postulates to be present
in anarthrous mass and plural NP such as *beer* and *linguists*

(see Fiengo (1974) for more discussion of this hypotethical null article). [Spec, $Q^1$] is taken to comprise the degree particles, *er*, *too*, *as*, *so*, etc; *more* being derived from *er much* and *less* and *fewer* from *er little* and *er few*, respectively.

On the subject of [Spec, $A^1$], however, she departs from Chomsky's speculations and from the work of previous lexicalist writers. Whereas Bowers (1970) and Selkirk (1970) analyze such expressions as *as tall* as having the degree particle *as* as the contents of [Spec, $A^1$], Bresnan provides a different analysis, to which we shall turn shortly, of degree particles that precede adjectives and adverbs. What she identifies as [Spec, $A^1$] is rather the class of adverbial intensifiers including *merely*, *utterly*, *perfectly*, *rather*, *quite*, etc.

She also suggests a change in the interpretation of the [Spec, $X^m$] notation. Instead of taking it as designating a category, that is, a node, she suggests taking it as being an abbreviation for the categories expanded in its position. She omits [Spec, $X^1$] nodes from her trees, and has the material expanded in these positions dominated by Det in NP and QP nodes, and by Adv in AP nodes. I shall follow these conventions.

Hence we attain the following series of analogously constructed phrases:

(2)  a.  *a man:*

$$N^2$$
```
        N²
      /    \
   Det      N¹
    |        |
    a       man
```

b.  *beer*
```
        N²
      /    \
   Det      N¹
    |        |
    ∅       beer
```

c.  *too much*
```
        Q²
      /    \
   Det      Q¹
    |        |
   too      much
```

d. *utterly crazy:*

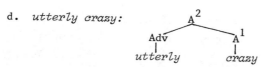

In these structures I have omitted the $X^0$ nodes, and will consistently do so when they play no role in the discussion.

Bresnan's proposal for degree modification of AP and quantity modification of NP is based on her observation of how degree modification of QP works. She observes that in such examples as (3):

(3) a. (much less) tall

b. (many (too many)) marbles

the phrasing is as indicated by the parentheses.

Bresnan explains the phrasing by reanalysing QP, AP and NP as $Q^3$, $A^3$ and $N^3$, respectively. The examples of (3) are thus given the structures (4):

(4) a.

b.

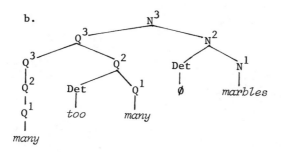

Justification for the constituent structure (4b) is given in the form of a rule of QP Shift (pg. 290) which derives (5) from (3b) by shifting $Q^2$ around $N^2$:

(5) many marbles too many.

This rule may be formulated as (6):

(6) *QP Shift:*

$$Q^3 \quad - \quad Q^2 \quad - \quad N^2 \qquad \text{OPT}$$

$$\begin{array}{ccc} 1 & 2 & 3 \\ 1 & \emptyset & 3\#2 \end{array} \implies$$

Note that this rule as formulated can misapply rather spectacularly. It can, for example, derive *she gave [many] [many]$_{NP}$[too many marbles]$_{NP}$* from *she gave [many]$_{NP}$ [too many marbles]$_{NP}$.* I will propose conventions to block this and other misapplications. Given the generally well-founded prohibition against moving nonconstituents, the argument for the phrasing indicated in (40b) is immediate.

We thus arrive at the following phrase structure rule:

(7) $X^3 \longrightarrow (Q^3) \; X^2$

An example of a $Q^3$ preceding a [Spec, $A^1$] is *he is less crazy than she is.*

We can see that when applied in AP, (7) will yield in addition to the grammatical outputs like (3a) the ungrammatical output of (8):

(8)  a. *as much intelligent

b. *too much intelligent

c. *that much intelligent.

A rule deleting *much* before $A^2$ would derive from (8) the grammatical (9), thereby providing a source for degree modification of AP:

(9)  a. as intelligent

b. too intelligent

c. that intelligent.

There is a difficulty, however, alluded to in Bresnan's footnote 4, in that while most adjectives, such as *tall*, reject overt *much:* *much tall;* some, like *different,* accept it: *much different.* Similar to *different* are a large class of what one might call intrinsically comparative adjectives are not in this class: *much similar*; and some that are not comparative, such as *aware* and *amused*. I am indebted to Wayles Brown for pointing out to me that an inordinate number of these adjectives begin with the prefix *a-*.

We find the following sample paradigms:

(10) a. *much intelligent

     b. *little intelligent

     c. as (*much) intelligent

     d. *as little intelligent

     e. more intelligent

     f. less intelligent

(11) a. much alike

     b. little alike

     c. as (much) alike

     d. as little alike

     e. more alike

     f. less alike

From (10), we glean that *intelligent* disdains to be preceded by $Q^0$: both *much intelligent* and *little intelligent* are bad, but whenever *much* Deletion applies, or the rule applies that permutes *er* around a following $Q^0$, then the examples are good. *alike* in (11), on the other hand, appears to be devoid of this restriction. Both *much alike* and *little alike* are grammatical.

Bresnan proposes to deal with ordinary adjectives by having *much* Deletion be obligatory, suggesting in footnote 4 that the rule is optional with such adjectives as *alike* and *different*. But this runs afoul of the fact that ordinary adjectives reject *little* as firmly as they reject *much*, without rejecting *less* and *more*. The facts concerning *little* would seem to call for a surface(y) filter ruling out *little A* sequences. But then it is strange that for all adjectives that are exceptions to the filter, *much* Deletion is optional.

These considerations plainly show that in fact *much*
Deletion is always optional, and that it is the surface
filter that is governed. For it presumably costs less in
features to specify the category $Q^0$ than to specify its
member *little*, and therefore the filter motivated by the
nonappearance of the *little A* sequences will be a *$Q^0A$
filter rather than a **little A* filter.

We can find further support for this position by noting
that ordinary adjective phrases such as *tall* and *intelligent*
are not ambiguous between their ordinary senses and a sense
in which they mean 'very tall' or 'very intelligent' (under
normal intonation and stress). Therefore, a derivation
from *much tall* to *tall* or from *much intelligent* to *intelli-*
*gent* by *much* Deletion is not possible. *much* Deletion can
only apply when *much* is preceded by its degree particle.
Nonetheless, we find **much tall*, **much intelligent*. Since
these forms cannot be blocked by turning them into something else with an obligatory transformation, we need a
filter to rule out *much A* sequences as well as *little A*
sequences. Both of these effects, as well as the apparent
obligatoriness of *much* Deletion with ordinary adjectives,
can be accomplished with a lexically governed filter on
$Q^0A$ sequences.

Further support for this analysis may be found by considering the behaviour of *enough:* **enough tall, tall*
*enough, enough alike, alike enough.* *Enough* permutes
obligatorily around ordinary adjectives, but optionally
around those which can be preceded by *much* and *little*.
Given Bresnan's conclusion that *enough* is a Q, this is what
we predict.

I will now formulate some rules. *much* Deletion I
formulate as follows:

(12) *much* Deletion:

| Det | - | *much* | - | $A^1$ | | OPT |
|-----|---|--------|---|-------|---|-----|
| 1 | | 2 | | 3 | | $\Longrightarrow$ |
| 1 | | $\emptyset$ | | 3 | | |

The reader will first note that the rule as formulated can

misapply in a way analogous to that pointed out for (6),
misderiving *too stale bread* from *too much stale bread*.
This problem will be solved by a constraint on rule application.

Another problem is term 3.  Its category features pose
no difficulties:  they are needed to block *too more bread*
and **as soup*, etc.  The superscript presents serious problems.  Consider the pair *very much so,* **very so,* pointed
out to me by Ross.  I shall want to analyse *so* in such
phrases as having the form (13):

(13)

We cannot, therefore, let (12) specify merely category
features without bars.  Given that bars must be specified,
3 is plainly wrong and 2 is against the evidence just cited.
My choice of 1 rather than 0 is arbitrary and descriptively
inconsequential.

This solves the descriptive problem, but the explanatory problem remains.  If we could find a principle determining a rule with superscript 1 in the last term on the
basis of data like *too tall,* **too more corn,* we would
explain *very much so,* **very so* rather than merely describe
it.  At present I have no such principle.  The reader will
also note that *too utterly crazy,* **too much utterly crazy*
presents a descriptive problem for (12), suggesting, con-
trary to *very much so,* **very so,* that the superscript on
term 3 should be 2 rather than 1.  I shall meet this problem
eventually, but for the present shall defer treatment of it.

The other problem is term 1.  Its effect is to block
the derivation of *tall* from *much tall*.  The problem is how
it is learned.  In order to require it to be in the rule,
one must specify in the data that the string *tall* lacks
*much tall* as an underlying structure.  It is very unclear
where this information might come from.  Perhaps having *tall*
ambiguous between *tall* and *much tall* is a universally un-
acceptable form of ambiguity, and grammars producing such
ambiguity for sentences in the basic data are automatically

discarded. Such a constraint on ambiguity might also explain while the rule deletes only *much* instead of both *much* and *little* (since the category $Q^0$ is closed, we cannot invoke recoverability of deletions, lest pronoun drop be made an impossible rule).

Finally, the optionality of the rule is no problem, given *too much alike*, etc. in the data.

The innocuous seeming rule of *much* Deletion has proved upon close examination to be rife with explanatory problems. This suggests that efforts should be directed towards eliminating it. I shall nonetheless retain the rule in the present work.

I now consider the rule permuting *er* around $Q^0$. The problem is to get this rule to keep the filter from throwing out *more intelligent* and *less intelligent*. If we suppose that the only kind of adjunction available is Chomsky adjunction, then the only way to do this is to adjoin *er* to $Q^1$:

(14)  *er* Shift

$$er - Q^1$$

$$\overset{\text{OBL}}{\Longrightarrow}$$

$$\begin{array}{cc} 1 & 2 \\ \emptyset & 2\#1 \end{array}$$

(14) will derive (15b) from (15a):

(15)  a.

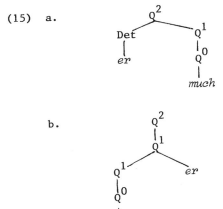

b.

One will note from (15) that I intend a derived constituent

128

structure convention whereby it is the node mentioned that
is moved, with nodes exhaustively dominating it vanishing,
as does the Det node in (15a).  This kind of application is
not possible within the formalization of Peters and Ritchie
(1973), although it is possible in Ginsburg and Partee
(1969).   Note that although these latter authors do not
provide for Chomsky adjunction, this could be amended.  The
rule can be gotten to be obligatory by the presumption that
OBL is a cheaper marking than OPT (or is the unmarked
instance).

Now for the filter.  Since the filter is lexically
governed, I shall assume that it must involve the category
$A^0$.  We may thus notate it as (16):

(16)  $Q^0$  $A^0$ Filter:

$*Q^0$  $A^0$

We may observe the usual form of misapplication:  the filter
as it stands will star *many old people* and *we gave many
stale bread*.  This problem will shortly be remedied.

Suppose then that the rules (including the filter) are
cyclic, and that rules cycle on $X^3$ nodes.  Then *er* Shift
will automatically apply before *much* Deletion and the
filter.  If we suppose in addition (as will turn out to be
necessary) that filters are extrinsically ordered with
respect to the rules, then the grammaticality of *too tall*
will force us to order the filter after *much* Deletion.  The
rules with these orderings will then suffice to deliver the
facts of (10-11).  I think that it is furthermore reasonable to believe that given a metatheory with transformations
and filters of the form indicated, the data of (10-11),
taken to be a pairing of each string with the set of its
deep structures, determines the analysis consisting of (12,
14, 16), excepting the problem of the superscript on term
3 of (12).

None of these rules are formulated with end-variables,
since there is nothing in (10-11) that motivates end-variables.  Nonetheless, we want the rules to apply as if they
had end-variables:  we want *er* Shift to derive *much more*

*intelligent* from *much er much intelligent*, we want *much*
Deletion to derive *much too intelligent*, and we want the
filter to block *much too much intelligent*. We may achieve
this effect by supposing that there is a convention that
automatically supplies end-variables to rules. Alterna-
tively, we might suppose that there is a requirement on the
form of rules that they have end variables:  then (12, 14,
16) would have to be replaced by their variants with end-
variables.  In either case, the rules motivated by (10-11)
would then apply in the desired manner in the more complex
examples given above.

   I will now formulate the rule deriving *taller* from
*more tall*.  At the beginning of the $A^3$ cycle, the structure
of taller will be (17):

(17)

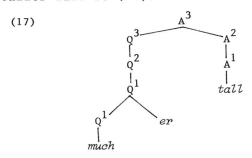

The simplest rule in our theory that could effect the
required change is (18):

(18) *more* Shift:

$$much \quad - \quad er \quad - \quad A^0$$

$$\text{OBL} \atop \Longrightarrow$$

$$1 \qquad\quad 2 \qquad\quad 3$$

$$\emptyset \qquad\quad \emptyset \qquad\quad 3\#2$$

Note that we would have to assume it to be in the basic
data that *taller* is not underlain by *less tall*.  I presume
that because the rule is governed by the adjective, term 3
must have the superscript 0.

   We may now show the assumption that the rules are
strictly ordered does some work.  Consider the underlying
structure of *too much taller*:

130

(19)

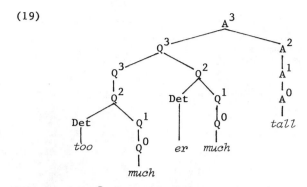

On the second $Q^3$ cycle in (19) we apply *er* Shift, and subsequently on the $A^3$ cycle we apply *more* Shift, yielding the
derived constituent structure (20):

(20)

Since *too much taller* is acceptable, and *tall* is not an
exception to the filter, we see that the application of the
filter must precede that of *more* Shift. We have already
noted, on the other hand, that *much* Deletion must precede
the filter. We therefore deduce by transitivity of ordering that *much* Deletion precedes *more* Shift. This is independently evidenced by the fact that \**too taller*, is ungrammatical. The assumption of strict ordering in conjunction with the preceding data thus predicts \**too taller*.

On the other hand, no evidence can be found for ordering
*er* Shift. Hence we arrive at an analysis consisting of the
following rules:

(21)  a.  *er* Shift          OBL   (14)

    b.  *much* Deletion       OPT   (12)

    c.  $*Q^0 \ A^0$ Filter         (16)

    d.  *more* Shift          OBL   (18)

The rules are assumed to apply cyclically.  The reader will
be able to discern that this assumption is not necessary
for the present data, and that the analyses of this section,
2.1, can be cast into a noncyclic framework.  I shall nonetheless assume cyclicity because of its greater elegance.
Assuming cyclicity, we shall soon see that a principle of
strict cyclicity is necessary.  But first it will be
necessary to give another constituent structure rule.

Bresnan finds that not only QP, but also AP appear as
predeterminer modifiers of QP, AP and predicative NP:

(22)  a.  far more people

    b.  as good an answer

    c.  as obviously good an answer

    d.  far too tall a man

We may thus replace (7) with (23):

(23)  $X^3 \longrightarrow \left\{ \begin{matrix} Q \\ A \end{matrix} \right\}^3 X^2$

(21) and (23) will assign to example (22d) the structure
(24):

(24)

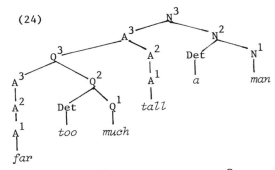

Note that $N^3$ with initial $A^3$ have a substantially different distribution from those with initial $Q^3$ or Det:
hence the designation predicative NP.  Their properties
are discussed by Bresnan (pg. 283, 299) and by Berman
(1974), who offers a rather different analysis.  Further-

more, observe that the contents of Det determine what can precede it under $X^3$:  in the QP system, for example, only *er* and *too* allow predeterminer QP; in the NP system, only the indefinite and null articles permit any sort of pre-determiner modification:

(25)  a.  *as good the answer
      b.  *more the men

We may now consider the question of strict cyclicity. Consider (26):

(26)  a.  as much better an answer
      b.  *as better an answer

(26a) will be underlain by (27a), which at the end of the $A^3$ cycle will have the derived structure (27b):

(27)  a.

      b.

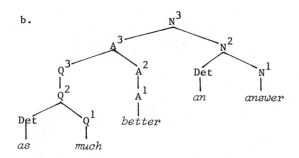

We must keep the filter from ruling out (26a), and *much* Deletion from generating (26b) from (27b).  A principle of strict cyclicity would accomplish this, since the first crack that the rules get at applying is on the $A^3$ cycle, where the extrinsic ordering keeps them in line.  Then

when we get to the $N^3$ cycle, strict cyclicity will keep
them from working, since they would have to operate entirely
within the $A^3$ domain that has already been cycled on.

A conventional formulation of a principle of strict
cyclicity would stipulate that a rule not apply entirely
within a domain that has already been cycled on. I will
put forth a different formulation, combining strict cyclicity with a principle that blocks a class of misapplications that we have been noting in the preceding pages.

I list these misapplications below:

(28)  a.  QP Shift (6):

*she gave [many]$_{NP}$ [too many marbles]$_{NP}$* —→ *she gave*

*[many]$_{NP}$ [marbles too many]$_{NP}$*

b.  *much* Deletion (12):

*too much stale bread* —→ *too stale bread*

c.  $Q^0$ $A^0$ Filter (16):

blocks *many old people, we gave many stale bread*

We may also note that *more* Shift will derive **I am angrier*
*than sad* from *I am more angry than sad* (see Bresnan pg. 327,
and, for a different account, Ross (1974). Hankamer (1973)
discusses similar sentences in Greek and Latin).

In all of these misapplications, we find that the rule
applies so that all of its constant terms (terms specified
as constituents) lie within domains that have already been
cycled on. For example in (28b) we have the structure
$[_N3[_Q3$ too much$][_N2[_A3$ stale$][_N1$ bread$]]]$ (I am not sure
of the internal constituent structure of the NP). When
*much* Deletion applies, the disappearing *much* and its Det
lie within the $Q^3$, and the $A^1$ *stale* lies within the $A^3$.
Both of these domains have already been cycled on.

I thus suggest the following principle which subsumes
both Strict Cyclicity and what is needed to block these
misapplications:

(29)  Cyclical Novelty Principle:

The structural description of a cyclical rule is
not met unless at least one of its constant terms
lies in a domain that has not yet been cycled on.

Observe that this principle would keep from applying a
Dative rule that mentioned only the two NP terms.  An
additional term, such as the verb, would have to be mentioned in order for the rule to ever get to apply.  Likewise, rules of Raising into subject and object positions
would have to mention some term in the matrix, such as the
verb.  These results seem reasonable.

Further note that the behaviour of QP Shift and *more*
Shift could be accommodated by a constraint against insertion into cyclical domains.  It is *much* Deletion and the
filter that necessitate a principle like (29).

The necessity for (29) is explanatory rather than descriptive.  We could build the effects of (29) into our
rules by appropriately deploying brackets within them.  For
example, she formulates *much* Deletion as follows (Bresnan's
example (10)):

(30)  Bresnan's *much* Deletion:

$$much \longrightarrow \emptyset \ / \ [... \ --A]_{AP}$$

(But c.f. Bresnan's fn. 5)

Given the present metatheory and the discussion of the
preceding pages, I would recast (30) as (31):

(31)  $[_A3 \ W_1 - Det - much - A^1]$ OPT $\Longrightarrow$

$$
\begin{array}{cccc}
1 & 2 & 3 & 4 \\
1 & 2 & \emptyset & 4
\end{array}
$$

But there is nothing in the basic data of (10-11) that
requires the outer $A^3$ brackets to be there.  The simplest
rule for that data will lack them.  Hence a theory with
(29) will explain why *too stale bread* is not derived from
*too much stale bread*, while in a theory without (29) one
can only describe the fact.

In this subsection, I have revised Bresnan's analysis
of the basic structures of QP, AP and adjectival NP, and

provided some reason to believe that the analysis is determined for the data by the metatheory, given some assumptions
about the form of the latter.  I have also shown the
explanatory significance of the assumption of strict ordering of transformations and filters, the convention supplying
end variables, and an extension of Strict Cyclicity, the
Cyclical Novelty Principle.  The discussion has finally
revealed that the rule of *much* Deletion is from an explanatory point of view the weakest part of the analysis, inasmuch as the least plausible assumptions about the basic
data are required to make it take its descriptively correct
form.  It would be a vindication of the methods of this
chapter should it prove desirable on independent grounds to
dispense with this rule.

2.1.2 *AP Shift:*  I here examine the process of AP Shift
discussed in Bresnan (1.5-1.6).  My goal will be to collapse Bresnan's AP Shift rule with the rule of QP Raising
that Bresnan postulates to crucially feed it, but does not
formulate.  I shall here ignore much of the original data
considered by Bresnan, especially taking no notice of any
facts connected with *such*.  *such* will be treated in the
next subsection.

The attentive reader may have noticed a difficulty with
the analysis of 2.1.1, in the form of paradigms like (32):

(32)  a.  as good a reply
      b.  *an as good reply
      c.  *better a reply
      d.  a better reply

Bresnan proposes to accommodate (32) by a rule of AP Shift
to which I shall give the preliminary formulation (33):

(33)  AP Shift (preliminary):

$$[_N3 \; A^2 \; - \; Det \; - \; N^1] \quad OBL \implies$$

$$1 \quad\quad 2 \quad\quad 3$$
$$\emptyset \quad\quad 2 \quad\quad 1\#3$$

(33) will derive (32d) from (32c), but not (32b) from (32a).
To see this, consider (34a), the structure of (32a) at the

beginning of the $N^3$ cycle, and (34b), the structure of (32c) at the beginning of the $N^3$ cycle:

(34) a.

b.

The QP remnant *as* in (34a) prevents there from being an $A^2$ initial in $N^3$, as required by the outer brackets of (33). On the other hand, in (34b), the QP that was initial in underlying structure has been destroyed by transformations, the *coup de grâce* having been administered by *more* Shift. Therefore (33) applies, deriving (32d).

(33) was picked arbitrarily from many other formulations that would have sufficed. Our next example will lead us to a reformulation that is almost uniquely determined. Consider (35):

(35) a. as much better a reply
     b. *an as much better reply
     c. ?? much better a reply
     d. a much better reply

Blocking (35b) is no problem: as (33) is currently formulated, it will not derive (35b) from (35a). The problem is to generate (35d) and block (35c). By the end of the $A^3$ cycle on (36a), the deep structure of (35d), the rules of (21) will have produced (36b):

(36)  a.

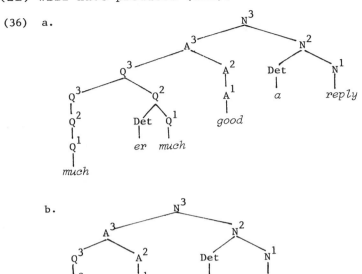

  b.

(36b) does not meet the structural description of (33).

But suppose we had a rule that would attach the initial QP *much* to the $A^2$ *better*:  then (33) would be able to apply, deriving (35d). This attachment rule is the QP Raising process. The process will cost less if we can collapse it with AP Shift. We therefore examine the latter more closely.

In the (33) formulation of AP Shift, it is assumed that the $A^2$ has to move around a Det. We find, however, that what can appear in the Det position after an AP is comple- tely determined:  if the NP is count singular, *a* must appear, otherwise the construction is impossible:  **as good* *beer*,  **too good the beer*, etc. This suggests that the Det position in this construction is syntactically empty, bearing the features [± sing, ± count], determined by the head N.  *a* is substituted by a transformation for a Det that is [+sing +count]. Later in the section I will deal with what happens when the combination of features in Det is otherwise. There are two things we need with regard to the hypothesis that the indefinite article here is underly-

ing null.  First, we want some independent evidence that
it is true, and second we want some principle to make it
true.  These will be provided later in the discussion.  For
the present, I shall show what can be done with the assumption that the Det is underlying null.

Given the underlying nullity of the Det of N in examples
like (32) and (35), we may simplify (33) by eliminating
from it term 2 and ordering it before the $a$-Insertion rule
(Note that since by assumption the rules have to be put in
some order, the particular order one puts them in is free).
Next, we will obviously want to have more general category
specifications than A and N for the two surviving terms.

Our rule will thus have the general form of (37):

(37)  $[_X3 \; Y^m - X^n]$  $\overset{OBL}{=\!\!\!\Rightarrow}$

      1     2

      $\emptyset$    1#2

It remains to identify $m$ and $n$.  $n = 3$ and $n = 2$ are clearly
out of the question, because then the rule could not effect
permutation over the empty Det.  $n = 0$ is also wrong because
then the shifted material would form a compound word with
the N (being Chomsky-adjoined to $N^0$), and the stress shows
that this is not what is happening.  We see thus that $n = 1$.

To determine $m$ is a little trickier.  Consider (38), the
structure of (35a) at the beginning of the $N^3$ cycle:

(38)

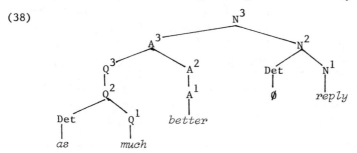

$m = 3$ we already know is wrong.  $m = 2$ is also wrong, for
on the $A^3$ cycle we would have been able to attach the $Q^2$
*as much* to the $A^1$ *better*, and then on the $N^3$ cycle we could
attach the resulting $A^1$ *as much better* to the $N^1$, thereby
generating (35b), **an as much better reply*, by subsequent

article insertion.    We are left with two possibilities:
$m = 1$, and $m = 0$.    Either would suffice.    I shall assume
$m = 1$, perhaps on the basis of a principle that high superscripts are cheaper than low.

The rule determined for (32, 35) is thus (39):

(39)  $X^1$ Attachment:

$$[_{Y}3 \ X^1 \ - \ Y^1] \quad \begin{array}{c} \text{OBL} \\ \Longrightarrow \end{array}$$

$$\begin{array}{cc} 1 & 2 \\ \emptyset & 1\#2 \end{array}$$

The only feature of (39) that is not determined by the data
is the superscript on term 1.    This is not really essential,
and I have proposed a principle that would cause it to be
determined also.

If we order $X^1$ Attachment after *er* Shift and before Indefinite Article Insertion, it will derive (35d) from its
deep structure (36a).    Below I give the derivation, circl-
ing that node in each derived tree that was being cycled on
to produce the tree from its predecessor, and boxing the
node that will be cycled on to produce the next.    Indefinite
Article Insertion is abbreviated on the final tree.

(40)  a.

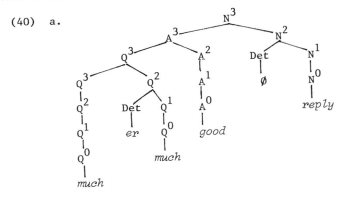

*er* Shift

b.

$X^1$ Attachment

c.

*more* Shift

d.

$X^1$ attachment

e.

$X^1$ Attachment

f.

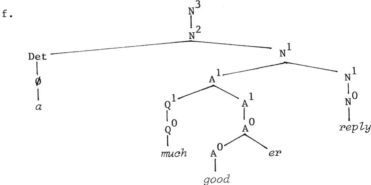

Note that with regard to the $A^3$ cycle (stages c and d) the rules of *more* Shift and $X^1$ Attachment could be applied in the reverse order without aborting the derivation. Likewise, the ordering with the $Q^0 A^0$ Filter and with *much* Deletion is immaterial.

The reader can easily verify that the rules will not derive (35b) from (38), but rather (38) will surface as (35a). Likewise, the rules can be seen to produce the correct results for paradigm (32). One aspect of the derivation (40) that may cause readers to balk is the $[_{Q^1} Q^1 Q^1]$ derived constituent structure in (40c). This is the structure which *much more* in *a much more intelligent answer* would have. This rather unnatural result will be eliminated in 2.1.3. For the present, we may merely observe that it is produced by the metatheory.

The present system of rules may be summarized as follows:

(41)  a.  *er* Shift                          OBL   (14)

     b.  $X^1$ Attachment                   OBL   (39)

     c.  Indefinite Article Insertion   OBL   (unformulated)

     d.  *much* Deletion                  OPT   (12)

     e.  $Q^0 A^0$ Filter                      (16)

     f.  *more* Shift                    OBL   (18)

These rules are hopefully a minimum set for data like (10, 11, 32, 35), although some of the superscripts are doubtful.

$X^1$ Attachment automatically incorporates the special feature of QP Raising noted by Bresnan that it will not incorporate a QP into a QP whose Det is nonnull:

(42)  a.  much too hard a job

     b.  *a much too hard job.

(42a) will be underlain by (43):

(43)

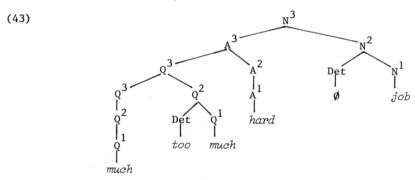

On the two $Q^3$ cycles, nothing will happen:  in particular, $X^1$ Attachment will not apply on the second $Q^3$ cycle because of the degree particle *too* intervening between the two $Q^1$ nodes.  Then on the $A^3$ cycle, *much* Deletion will apply, but again $X^1$ Attachment will be blocked.  Finally, $X^1$ Attachment will yet again be blocked on the $N^3$ cycle. Hence the formulation of $X^1$ Attachment determined by the simpler cases automatically extends to the case of (42).

I will now motivate an additional filter in the analysis.

Consider (44-46):

 (44) a. as good a linguist

    b. *as good linguists

 (45) a. *as good linguists

    b. better linguists

 (46) a. *as good beer

    b. better beer

In precisely those examples where $X^1$ attachment will succeed in attaching $A^1$ to $N^1$, thereby destroying $A^3$ and $A^2$, the example is good. Otherwise it is bad. We may suppose then that there is a filter following article insertion that prohibits $A^2 N^1$ (or equivalently, $A^3 N^1$) sequences. The formulations of the $*A^2 N^1$ filter and the article insertion rules are trivial.

We may now consider an apparent counterexample:

 (47) a more utterly crazy lunatic

By our rules, the underlying structure for (47) would have to be (48):

 (48)

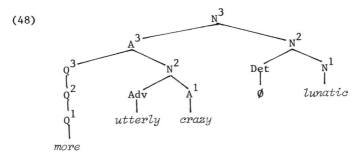

The Adv *utterly* will block $X^1$ Attachment on its attempt to apply to the circled $A^3$, so that *more utterly crazy a lunatic* will be derived, and the grammatical form will not be. This is precisely consonant with the problem we noted in the preceding subsection of the grammaticality of *too utterly crazy*, in which *much* Deletion is applying before *utterly* (recall *too \*(much) so*, etc.).

I propose that in these examples *utterly* is an ordinary A rather than an Adv. (47) will not then have (48) as its structure, but will rather have a structure parallel to *a more obviously crazy lunatic.*

I now return to the cyclicity principle (29). Strict Cyclicity principles are characteristically thought of as prohibiting operations entirely within a domain dominated by a cyclic node. This leaves open the question of what happens if the cyclic node dominating a domain is removed. We can see that in the case of (29), the newly exposed material should not be resubmitted to rule application. Consider *a much better linguist.* This is derived from $X^1$ Attachment from *much better a linguist.* $X^1$ attachment removes the $A^3$ node from over *much better,* yet the $Q^0$ $A^0$ Filter does not get a chance to rule the sentence out on the $N^3$ cycle.

We can formalize (29) appropriately by introducing into a theory a division between red and green brackets. The base produces structures in which all the brackets are green. When the cycle on a domain is finished, all the brackets (including the outermost) on that domain are painted red. (29) then becomes a constraint that one of the factors covered by a constant term in a rule must contain green brackets in order for the structural description of the rule to be met. I believe that this formalism could be extended to the treatment of idioms given by Kiparsky (1975).

We are finally left with the problem of the indefinite article. The following data can be taken to support either a rule of *one(s)* Deletion or a rule of *one(s)* Insertion (I am indebted to Hankamer for pointing this out to me):

(49)  a.  I wrecked Bill's old car, and you wrecked
          Harry's new *(one).

      b.  I wrecked Bill's car, and you wrecked Harry's
          (*one).

(50)  a.  I bought three old records, and you bought three
          new *(ones).

b.  I bought three records, and you bought four

   (*ones).

We could say that *one(s)* is deleted after quantifiers and
possessives, or inserted after adjectives (but note *this
one* and *that one*:  I suspect that this is a different *one*)
   Observe the following contrast:

(51)   a.  Bill is a piano player and Lucinda is one too.

       b.  Bill is as good a piano player as Dinu Lapitti,
           and Lucinda is as good a one as Horowitz.

Perlmutter (1970) suggests that the indefinite article is
a stressless form of the numeral *one*, and that there is
deletion of the identity-of-sense pronoun *one* after numerals, including the indefinite article.  Hence the predicate
nominal *one* in (51a) is analysed as underlyingly *one one*,
with the second *one* disappearing by *one(s)* Deletion.

   But this approach cannot explain the appearance of *a
one* in (51b).  Even if the *a* were underlying empty, so
that we had a structure like (52)

(52)

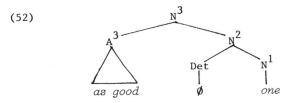

a *one(s)* Deletion rule would still apply, providing that
the null Det were of the same grammatical category as a
numeral, since terms of transformations can take null
factors.

   But suppose instead that *one(s)* is inserted, presumably
for an empty $N^0$.  We might formulate the rule as follows:

(53)  *one(s)* Insertion

$A^3$ -- $N^0$
                      OBL

1        2        $\Longrightarrow$

1        PRO

Then the appearance of *ones* in (51b) is explained, as long
as *one(s)* Insertion follows Indefinite Article Insertion.

I have formulated the rule as insertion of PRO rather than as insertion of *one(s)* because I wish to preserve the solution proposed in Andrews (1974) to the problem presented in (54):

(54)  a.  I ate Bill's meat and you ate Mary's.

b.  *I ate Bill's expensive meat and you ate Mary's cheap.

When the $N^0$ for which one would substitute *one(s)* is mass, nothing can be done.  I proposed that *one(s)* was inserted by surface structure lexicalization for a feature complex, and that there simply wasn't a lexical item that could be inserted for the mass counterpart to *one(s)*.  Derivations surfacing with unlexicalizable positions would then block. Thus if (53) inserts PRO into an $N^0$ that is [-count], there is no lexical item that can fill this position, and the derivation blocks, explaining the ungrammaticality of (54b).

We finally want a principle to force the indefinite article to be underlyingly null.  I propose the principle that if an $N^3$ is analysable as $A^3 N^2$, it is also analysable as $A^3 N^1$.  One would hope to derive this principle from more general considerations, presumably of semantic interpretation.

2.1.3  *So and Such*:  Bresnan (section 1.4) observes a mass of facts which support the notion that the AP Shift process is capable of moving an AP while stranding an associated *so*, which subsequently becomes *such*:

(55)  a.  so tall a man

b.  *so a tall man

c.  *such tall a man

d.  such a tall man

Observing in addition the following data:

(56)  a.  so much better a linguist

b.  *such a (much) better linguist

we are led to propose the following reformulation of $X^1$

Attachment that will accommodate the above data:

(57) $[_Y3 \langle so \rangle_1 - \begin{matrix} X \\ \langle +A \rangle_1 \end{matrix} {}^1 - Y^1]$

$\xRightarrow[\langle OPT \rangle_1]{}$

$\quad$ 1 $\qquad$ 2 $\qquad$ 3

$\quad$ 1 $\qquad$ $\emptyset$ $\qquad$ 2#3

In interpreting this rule, we can take OPT as a feature or
as a non-feature with regard to the angle bracket notation
If we take it as a non-feature, we want rules with no
specification to be obligatory;  if we take it as a featur
we want [-OPT] = OBL.  The rule has an equally highly
valued equivalent in which the role of '+A' is filled by
'-Q.'

(57) is, I believe, the minimal rule for the data we
have seen so far, but it is in fact incorrect, going badly
haywire in some rather intricate derivations.  Consider
(58b), the underlying structure of (58a):

(58)  a.  such an obviously more plausible suggestion

$\qquad$ b.

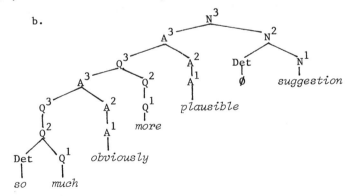

On the $A^3$ cycle, *much* Deletion will happen.  On the $Q^3$
cycle, *obviously* and *more* will glom together under $Q^1$,
resulting in the derived constituent structure (58c):

148

(58)   c.

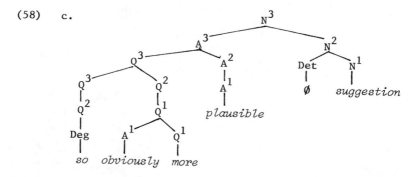

But now we are stuck.  To get to a stage where we can shift
*obviously more plausible* into the $N^2$, we have to attach the
$Q^1$ *obviously more* to the $A^1$ *plausible*, and this operation
is prohibited by the formulation of (57).

This formulation is necessary in order to avoid generating *(56b) from (56a).  To avoid the generation of *(56b),
we must block incorporation of a $Q^1$ that is preceded by *so*
into an $A^1$, and that is precisely what we must do in order
to progress from (58b) to the grammatical (58a).

It is not sufficient to merely change (57):  rather,
we must alter the metatheory so that it is not in fact
compatible with the data of the preceding section and that
of (55-56).

The rule of $X^1$ Attachment produces derived constituent
structures such as (59), which have doubtless upset many
readers when they have occurred in our derivations:

(59)   a.

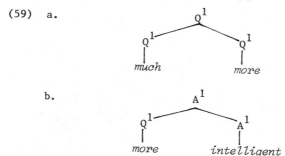

      b.

These structures have the property that the basic modifier-
head relationships have been obscured.  Let us then add to
the metatheory a stipulation that structures of the form
(60) cannot be produced by a transformation:

(60)

(where, of course, any of X, Y and Z may be equal to one another). We might accomplish this with a restriction that structures of the form (60) are obligatorily interpreted as coordinate structures.

The rule of $X^1$ Attachment (39) is no longer compatible with the data (32, 32), since it assigns to these sentences impossible derived constituent structures. I believe that instead of the minimal rule is (61):

(61)   $X^2$ Attachment (first try):

$$[_{Y}3 \ [_{X}2 \ X^1] - Y^1] \quad \underset{=\!=\!\rightarrow}{\text{OBL}}$$

$$1 \qquad 2$$

$$\emptyset \qquad 1 \# 2$$

$X^2$ Attachment, like $X^1$ Attachment, produces the additional facts of (42), as desired. We have thus not lost explanatory potency in this direction. We also, however, have attained intuitively far more comfortable derived constituent structures.

The derivation of *a much better reply* goes through as follows:

(62)   a.

150

b.

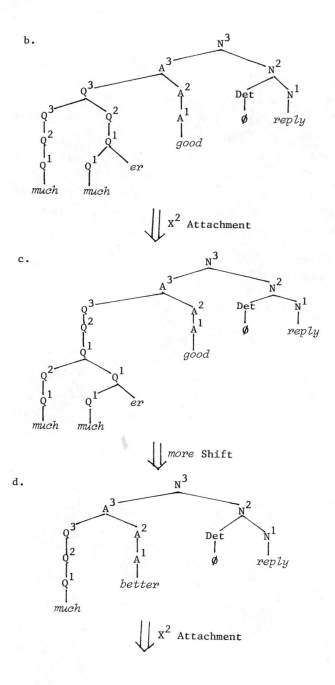

$X^2$ Attachment

c.

$more$ Shift

d.

$X^2$ Attachment

e.

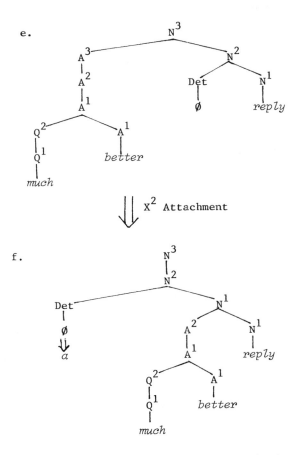

$X^2$ Attachment

f.

Now let us return to the data of (55). Given the revised metatheory and the data of the preceding sections, the minimal way to accommodate (55) is to reformulate $X^2$ Attachment as follows:

(63) $X^2$ Attachment (second try):

$$[_Y3 <so>_1 - [_{X}2 X^1] - Y^1] \qquad <OPT>_1$$
$$1 \qquad 2 \qquad 3 \qquad \Longrightarrow$$

$$1 \qquad \emptyset \qquad 2\#3$$

Now (63), unlike (57), automatically predicts the facts of (56b). The underlying structure of (56a) will be (64):

152

(64)

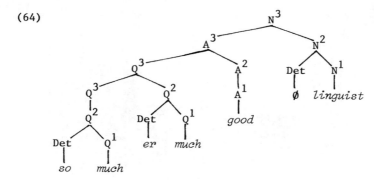

But (64) will never meet the structural description of the
new $X^2$ Attachment, so that the derivation to *(56b) will be
blocked. The reason the rule does not get to apply to (64)
is that the initial *so* is under the $Q^2$ of the $Q^1$ that
immediately follows it; while in (65), the underlying
structure of (55a), that $Q^1$ gets deleted on the $A^3$ cycle,
leaving *so* preceding $A^2$ on the $N^3$ cycle, so that (63) can
apply:

(65)

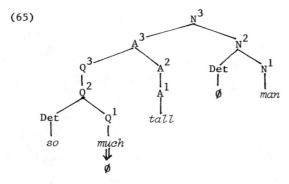

Going back to the example (58) (*so obviously plausible a
suggestion*), which defeated the original $X^1$ Attachment rule,
we find that the derivation by $X^2$ Attachment does not get
hung up. On the $A^3$ cycle *much* disappears, and then $X^2$
Attachment works smoothly on each following cycle.

The metatheoretical principle ruling out structures of
the form (60) thus results in very substantial explanatory
improvements: from the data of (55) are predicted both the
data of (56) and (58). The principle has the added appeal
of ruling out a constituent structure that is counter-
intuitive, to say the least.

We may note a pleasant by-product of the reformulation of the attachment rule: the filter to exclude *as good beer* receives unique characterization as an $*A^3 \, N^1$ filter. This is, of course, free beer rather than an argument.

We must finally extend the analysis in order to accommodate a few more facts brought forth by Bresnan. Consider such examples as the following:

(66)  a.  Bill is less a linguist than you are.

       b.  Ferdinand is too much a scholar to publish junk like that.

       c.  He has become more a poet than a linguist.

Bresnan assigns to *less a linguist* the structure (67) (after *er* Shift):

(67)

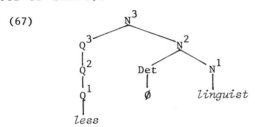

I would be inclined to have the $Q^3$ immediately dominated by $A^3$. This would capture the intuitive resemblance of these structures to the predeterminer adjective constructions, and explain *less a one* by *one(s)* Insertion, and *\*this is less beer than that* by the $*A^3 \, N^1$ filter.

Regardless of whether we make these emendations, rule (63) will misapply to (67), deriving *\*a less linguist*. Hence (63) must be again reformulated. (68) appears to do the job:

(68)  $X^2$ Attachment (final version):

$$[_{Y^3} \langle so \rangle_1 - [_{X^2} [_{\langle Q \rangle_2}^X]^1 ] - \begin{array}{c} Y \\ \langle -N \rangle_2 \end{array}^1 \quad \langle OPT \rangle$$

$$\begin{array}{cccc} 1 & 2 & 3 & \Longrightarrow :\to 1 \\ 1 & \emptyset & 2\#3 & \end{array}$$

Note how crucially this formulation relies on the differing interpretation of angle brackets around features (as in

154

term 2) and around nonfeatures (terms 1 and 3), as specified in Sound Patterns of English (p.394-395). Also note
that (68) merely describes, rather than explains, (66).

I list the salient rules in the analysis we have arrived at as follows:

(69)  a.  *er* Shift                OBL        (14)
      b.  $X^2$ Attachment          OBL        (68)
      c.  Ind. Art. Insertion       OBL        (unformulated)
      d.  $*A^2 N^1$ Filter                    (unformulated)
      e.  *much* Deletion           OPT        (12)
      f.  $*Q^0 A^0$ Filter                    (16)
      g.  *more* Shift              OBL        (18)

There are various further data and constructions considered
in Bresnan (1.5 - 1.6). The reader can verify that under
Bresnan's account of the underlying structures, the rules
of (69) work correctly. They also apply appropriately to
the indefinite superlative construction of Bresnan (1.7).

2.1.4  *The Indefinite Comparative:*  The indefinite comparative is the structure exemplified in the following examples:

(70)  a.  The more you work, the less you get
      b.  The taller you are, the heavier.
      c.  The more pizzas Mary eats, the fatter she gets.

My own work on these constructions is a reanalysis of
material covered in Thiersch (1974). I will here consider
the internal constituent structure of the preposed constituents in *the*: *the more pizza* and *the fatter* in (70c),
for example. The clausal relations will be discussed in
2.2.1, though it should be obvious that I am going to say
that the initial clause is an anticipatory clause like the
anticipatory relatives of the preceding chapter.

The problem is to determine the underlying constituent
of the *the*. Thiersch analyses it as a COMP, occurring
initially in each clause, which attracts the constituent
with *more* to it. The following examples, however, suggest
that it is instead an occupant of the Det of QP:

(71)  a.  The more you practice, the better a pianist
          you will be.

b.  The better a linguist you are, the fewer questions
you have to ask your informants.

Consider the phrases *the better a pianist, the better a
linguist*.  If the *the* is in COMP, nothing can explain the
ungrammaticality of *\*the a better linguist, \*the a better
pianist, \*the a more obviously competent insurance salesman*,
etc.  But suppose *the* is in the Det of QP.  Then *the better
a pianist* will have the underlying structure (72a), reaching the surface as (72b):

(72)   a.

      b.

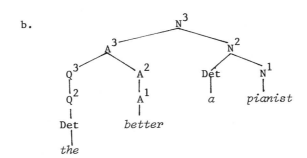

The $Q^3$ remnant *the* prevents $X^2$ Attachment from applying on
the $N^3$ cycle.

    This analysis further is confirmed when we see such
examples as *he tried all the harder, so much the worse for
him, he became all the better a psychologist for it*.  In
these cases the *the* is preceded by predeterminer material,
though it is not in the indefinite comparative construction.

    This little studied construction thus fits easily into
Bresnan's analysis.

2.2 *Comparative Clauses in the Base*:  I will here determine the underlying position of comparative clauses.  In
2.2.1 I examine and reject the traditional view that comparative clauses are generated in the Det of the QP they
modify.  In section 2.2.2 I propose that comparative
clauses (including the indefinite comparatives of (2.1.4)
are generated in the base in the positions that they occupy
on the surface, and indicate what the responsible rules
are.

2.2.1 *The Determiner Analysis*:  Bresnan (pp. 338-343)
proposes the traditional analysis of the underlying structure of comparative clauses, in which they are generated
within the Det of the QP they modify, and are then moved
to their surface position by rules of Comparative Formation
and Extraposition.  Hence (73) is underlain by (74), which
undergoes the movement indicated by the arrow, as well as
deletion of a constituent identical to the head except for
its special Determiner $x$ in the QP ($x$ is the symbol for the
Det of the 'target QP' of the comparative clause, rather
than a logical variable):

(74)

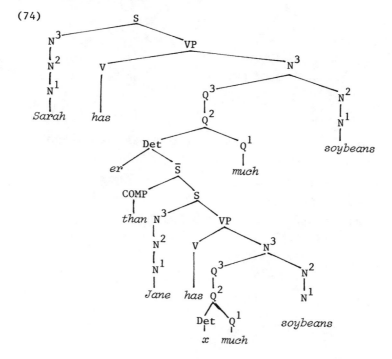

Bresnan cites two motivations supporting this structure. The first is that the cooccurrence restrictions between the COMP of the comparative clause and the Det of the modified QP may easily be stated over these structures. Bresnan observes that these restrictions hold over unbounded distances in surface structure (Bresnan p. 339):

(75)  a.  Mary doesn't have as many too many too many
          ... marbles as Jane.
      b.  Cindy has more nearly as many too many
          marbles as Julie than Linda

The second reason is that this structure allows a systematic explanation for the exclusion from the comparative clause of certain modifiers in the head, namely, those that precede the determiner with which the clause is associated. Consider, for example, (76):

(76)  Melvin sliced twice as many bagels as Seymour

We wish (76) to be derived from (77) rather than from (78):

(77)  Melvin sliced twice as [Seymour sliced x many bagels]
      many bagels

(78)  Melvin sliced twice as [Seymour sliced twice x many
      bagels] many bagels

Given determiner generation of the comparative clause, the modifiers that are excluded are given a straightforward characterization as those that are to the right of the clause itself in its underlying position.

To these considerations may be added a third, the support of semantic interpretation. The semantics of comparatives will obviously go more smoothly if there is some systematic representation of the relations between a comparative clause and the QP it modifies. Davis and Hellan (in preparation), for example, give a model theoretic semantics for comparatives that is based essentially on Bresnan's analysis, and assume that the comparative clause is generated in the determiner.

There are nonetheless many severe problems with determiner generation of comparative clauses. First, there are difficulties connected with formulating the rule.

The presumed derived constituent structure from the application of Comparative Formation to (74) is (79):

(79)

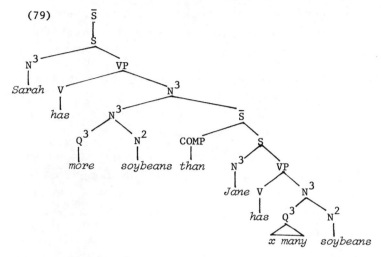

Bresnan suggests that Comparative Formation also effects deletion of the constituent *x many soybeans* in the comparative clause that is identical to the head (when the clause has been removed). I have omitted this feature in (79).

If (79) is the derived constituent structure produced by Comparative Formation, then the rule has to have the effect of Chomsky adjoining the comparative clause to its head, which is an operation of Chomsky adjoining a constitu ent to a containing constituent (and deleting the original occurrence within that constituent). Because the rule requires operations (deletion and adjunction) on overlapping domains, it is not formulable as a single transformation within the framework of Peters and Ritchie (1973) (cf. Peters and Ritchie p.54, p. 60 def. 210). I do not think one could easily introduce the capacity to perform such operations either into the Peters and Ritchie framework or the Partee and Ginsburg (1969) framework. One could probably find a way by factoring Comparative Formation into two successive operations, an adjunction and an erasure, but my best efforts in this direction are hardly attractive. The rule is thus unformulable as a single transformation in available formalisms, and the necessity

for factoring it into two transformations considerably
increases its cost and lowers its appeal.

Additional problems arise when we attempt to specify
where Comparative Formation is to put the clause it moves.
Bresnan (pp. 328-329) notes paradigms such as the following:

(80)  a.  Bill is more than five feet tall.

   b.  Bill is taller than five feet.

   c.  *Bill is more than Max (is) tall.

   d.  Bill is taller than Max (is).

She shows that the correct phrasing for the AP of (4a) is
*(more (than five feet)) tall*, and proposes that the comparative clause originates from an underlying equational sentence 'five feet is $x$ much.' She claims that the verb of
this sentence cannot be the copula, but must be a special
abstract equational predicate, but the basis for this is
not clear to me. The copula would appear to suffice in the
light of such examples as *five feet is more than six inches*,
etc.

We can thus propose (81) to underly (80):

(81)  a.  Bill is er [than five feet is $x$ much] much tall.

   b.  Bill is er [than five feet is $x$ much tall] much tall.

   c.  Bill is er [than Max is $x$ much] much tall.

   d.  Bill is er [than Max is $x$ much tall] much tall.

The comparative clause may in these examples be seen to be
attaching to that constituent in the head which is identical
to the disappearing constituent in the comparative clause.
(80c) is ungrammatical because putting the comparative
clause after *er much* forces the deleted constituent in the
comparative clause to be $x$ *much*, which cannot be equated
with *Bill*.

This sort of approach too breaks down because of
examples like the following:

(82)  a.  Bill sliced more salami than Harry did bologna.

   b.  The table is longer than the door is wide.

   c.  More men than women (did) made reservations.

   d.  He gave more cash than he did attention to his mistress.

The sources of these would be (83):

(83) a. Bill sliced er [than Harry sliced $x$ much bologna] much salami.

b. the table is er [than the door is $x$ much wide] much long

c. er [than $x$ many men made reservations] many women made reservations

d. he gave er [than he gave $x$ much attention to his mistress] much cash to his mistress

No condition on Comparative Formation stated in terms of identity can generate (82) but block (84):

(84) a. *Bill sliced more than Harry did bologna salami.

b. *The table is more than the door is wide long.

c. *More than women did men made reservations.

d. *He gave more than he did attention (to his mistress cash to his mistress.

Bresnan notes these problems, but does not give a clear solution.

The situation gets worse if we observe some restrictions found by Pinkham (1974). Pinkham noted that when a comparative clause was attached to its head, rather than extraposed, and neither contained a structure identical to the head nor was identical outside the head to the matrix, then the sentence was ungrammatical. Corresponding to the grammatical (82c, d) are the grammatical (85a, b) and the ungrammatical (86a, b):

(85) a. More men than I expected to made reservations.

b. Bill gave more cash than Maurice did to Brycelinde.

(86) a. *More men than I expected women to made reservations.

b. *Bill gave more cash than Maurice did affection to Brycelinde.

Conditions on a movement rule would appear to be an unlikely way to explain what comparative clauses go where.

Attempts to maintain a determiner source for comparative clauses are finally defeated by multiple headed comparatives like these:

(87)  As fair a woman and as foul a man as I have ever seen
together are coming toward us.

(88)  a.[2] People do crazier things at higher speeds on the
McGrath Highway than they do other places.

b.  Marcille gave a longer talk at a better attended
session than did her husband.

c.  Alfred bestowed a heartier kiss on a prettier girl
than Maxwell did.

Liberman (1974) also cites multiple headed result clauses:
*John hit his car so hard so many times with such a big
hammer than it finally started.*

(87) would presumably be underlain by (89), and (88) by
(90):

(89)  as much fair a woman and as much foul a man [as I have
ever seen x much fair a woman and x much foul a man
together] are coming toward us.

(90)  Alfred bestowed er much hearty a kiss on er much pretty
a girl [than Maxwell bestowed x much hearty a kiss on
x much pretty a girl]

The other examples of (88) have structures parallel to (90).
Note that the 'x' in these examples is not a logical variable, but a symbol for the abstract formative (*so?*) that
is the Det of the QP in the comparative clause.

One might think to generate (87) by generating a comparative clause in each conjunct of the coordinate NP, and
applying Right Node Raising, but the presence of *together*
renders this impossible: *I have ever seen x much fair a
woman together* is ungrammatical.  This result is preserved
under current theories in which many aspects of semantic
interpretation are determined from surface structure,
because in these theories Right Node Raising would have the
comparative clause binding traces in each conjunct, and
interpretation would use these to determine the meaning as
if the movement had not occurred (see Vergnaud 1974, pp.82-
83 for discussion).  We get the same result in (88) where
there aren't any processes that could yield the comparative

clause by combining well-formed clauses on the individual
matrix comparative determiners.

(87-88) might be dismissed as marginal phenomena.  If
they were the sole evidence against Comparative Formation,
one might still maintain the rule with a relatively clear
conscience.  But in the light of the preceding discussion,
which shows that the formulation of the rule is highly
problematic, if possible at all, they become telling
counterevidence.

There is a final consideration that we must discuss
before accepting (87-88) as counterevidence to Comparative
Formation.  There are sentences in natural language which
'sound all right' and suggest a meaning, but certainly
don't get their meaning by means of regular rules of
grammar.  For example, "the more you eat the more you want
the more you eat" suggests the presence of a vicious circle,
but it certainly doesn't do this by means of regular rules
of semantic interpretation.  Rather, the meaning is deliv-
ered iconically, by an operation of free intelligence.  One
might correspondingly claim that (87, 88) were not sentences of English, but rather surface patterns resembling
sentences, and receiving meanings not by regular rules but
by some vague sort of suggestiveness.

The only way to refute such a proposal is to give rules
for interpreting multiple headed comparatives, and show
that they fit in reasonably well with the rest of the
rules of semantic interpretation of the language.  The
semantics of comparatives is quite complicated, and that
of multiple headed comparatives much more so.  I wish to
spare the reader most of my presently rather ill thought
out ideas on the subject.  I will, however, bring forth
some reasons to believe that multiple headed comparatives
are interpreted in a reasonably disciplined fashion.

Postal (1974) suggested a semantics for comparatives
in which they were interpreted as two definite descriptions
connected by a relational predicate.  Hence "Bill has more
money than Tom" comes out "the amount of money Bill has
exceeds the amount of money Tom has."  Now consider an

experiment on the effects of marijuana smoking. We may say
"50 people smoked 100 joints" and mean either 50 people
smoked 100 joints apiece, or 50 people smoked 100 joints
between them (there are other readings, but they are not
very sensible in the given context). Now suppose we say
"more people smoked more joints in this experiment than in
the last." We might mean that the total number of partici-
pants in this experiment exceeded that in the last and the
total number of joints smoked in this experiment exceeded
that in the last, or we might mean that more people parti-
cipated and they each smoked more joints.

We can get this effect by introducing a definite description operator that denotes not an amount, but rather
an ordered pair of amounts, and likewise extending the
'exceeds' relation and the others to be relations over
ordered n-tuples rather than merely individuals. Our
example would thus have a logical structure like (91):

(91)   (A X, Y) (X people smoked Y joints in this experiment)
        exceeds (A X, Y) (X people smoked Y joints in the
        last experiment).

'A' is the operator forming definite descriptions of
amounts or n-tuples of amounts. I would interpret 'exceeds'
in '$(x_1,\ldots, x_n)$ exceeds $(y_1, \ldots, y_n)$' as meaning that for
$i = 1, \ldots, n$, $x_i$ exceeds $y_i$, but one might dissent from
this. The ambiguity in the example thus derives from the
ambiguity of 'X people smoked Y joints', which ambiguity
would presumably be eliminated in a reasonable semantic
representation. There is much more to be said on the
subject of multiple headed comparative semantics, but I
shall not try to say it here.

The above discussion, though incomplete, suffices to
show that structures like (87-88) are really sentences.
Their status as evidence is thereby confirmed.

2.2.2 *The Base Position of Comparative Clauses*:  The
comparative clauses that we have seen, including the double
headed ones, come in two surface positions:  attached to a
head, and extraposed. I shall propose underlying structures
for both in which the deep position is also the surface

position.   After examining the regular comparatives, I will
turn to the indefinite comparatives.

The crucial fact about headed comparatives is that they
can stack, and there is a constraint, which I call the
mirror-image constraint, that the clauses must appear in
the reverse order from that of the determiners of the QP
that they are associated with:

(92)   a.   As many more people than I invited as you predicted
            came to the party.

       b. *As many more people as you predicted than I invited
            came to the party.

Since they stack, I shall presume that they are introduced
by the rule $X^3 \longrightarrow X^3\ \bar{S}$.   When X = N, we get examples like
(92).   When X = A we get sentences like *the chair is twice
as much wider than the door as I expected*.   And when X = Q,
we get those like *the plants grow as much as six feet high*.

Extraposed comparatives also appear to stack, and to
obey the mirror-image constraint, even in conjunction with
embedded comparatives:

(93)   a.   As many more people than I invited came to the
            party as you predicted.

       b. *As many more people as you predicted came to the
            party than I invited.

       c.   As many more people came to the party than I
            invited as you predicted.

       d. *As many more people came to the party as I
            invited than you predicted.

By analogy with relative clauses, it would be reasonable to
propose that extraposed comparatives be introduced by the
$S \longrightarrow S\ \bar{S}$ rule that introduces extraposed relatives.

This rule leads us to expect to find comparative clauses
with a head in each conjunct of a coordinate S, but not of
a coordinate $\bar{S}$:

(94)   a.   More men were singing and more women were dancing
            than I had ever seen on a stage at once.

b.  Bill reported that more men were singing and (*that)
more women were dancing than he had ever seen on a
stage at once.

c.  than I/he had ever seen x many men and x many women on
a stage at once

(94a) illustrates the construction, (94b) shows that a
comparative clause cannot be attached to conjoined S̄, and
(94c) shows the presumed underlying structure for the comparative clauses in these examples.

We see that an extraposed comparative can precede or
follow an extraposed relative, and that the mirror-image
constraint appears to hold:

(95) a. More men came to the party who were drunk than I
expected would.

b. *More men came to the party than I expected would who
were drunk.

c. More men picked a girl up who was willing than we
expected

d. *More men picked a girl up than we expected who was
willing.

These facts strengthen the hypothesis.

Williams (1974) proposed that comparative and result
clauses extraposed to the end of the S that was their
scope.  Consider such examples as these:

(96) a.  Bill's teachers said he was so smart he could
solve any problem.

b.  Bill's teachers said he was smarter than anybody
else was.

c.  Bill's teachers said he was so smart that people
doubted their recommendations.

d.  Bill's teachers said he was smarter than anybody
else did.

In (96a, b), the scope of the comparative or result clause
is the complement sentence.  In (96a), Bill's problem
solving ability is said to be a consequence of how smart he
is, not how smart people say he is;  and in (96b) Bill is
said to be smarter than anybody else.  In (96c, d), however,

the scope of the comparative and result clauses is the
matrix. In (96c), it is the extent to which Bill's teachers say he is smart that causes disbelief, and in (96d),
the extent to which Bill's teachers say he is smart is
compared with the extent to which anybody else does.

Williams claims that these scope differences correspond to differences in surface constituent structure as
follows:

(97)  a.  Bill's teachers said [he was so smart he could
          solve any problem]
      b.  Bill's teachers said [he was smarter than anybody
          else was]
      c.  [Bill's teachers said that he was so smart] that
          people doubted their recommendations
      d.  [Bill's teachers said he was smarter] than anybody
          else did.

This claim is supported by the following contrasts involving the placement of matrix agent phrases:

(98)  a.  *Bill is said to be so smart by his teachers that
          he can solve any problem.
      b.  *Bill is said to know more by his teachers than
          anybody else does.
      c.  Bill was said to be so smart by his teachers that
          people doubted their recommendations.
      d.  Bill was said to be smarter by his teachers than
          he was by anybody else.

When the clause has scope within the complement, the matrix
agent phrase cannot be interpolated between it and its head.
Assuming that nodes cannot be moved into S by the rules
that position adverbs or prepositional phrases, the result
follows immediately from the bracketing of (97).

We can see that the clause may be indefinitely far
removed from its head by contemplating examples such as
*Bill is said by his friends.....to be believed by his
teachers to be smarter than anybody else is*, etc.

We can produce multiple headed examples precisely
parallel to (98):

(99)  a.  *People are said to do crazier things at higher
          speeds there by Dorothy than they do other places.

      b.  *People are said to do such crazy things at such high
          speeds there by Dorothy that they get killed off
          in droves.

      c.  People are said to do crazier things at higher speeds
          there by Dorothy than they are by other people.

      d.  People are said to do such crazy things at such high
          speeds there by Dorothy that I am getting skeptical.

It cannot be maintained, then, that comparative and result
clauses are extraposed to the end of the S that is their
scope.  Rather, they are base-generated in approximately
that area.  I propose that they are base-generated as
sisters to the S that is their scope.

Notice that we have here rather massive Right-Roof Constraint violations (assuming that the connections between
the clauses and their heads obey island constraints), but
that the sentential subject constraint is respected: *that
Seymour sliced so many bagels is obvious that his arm fell
off.  These results strengthen the suspicion voiced in
section 1.1.3.6 that the Right Roof Constraint should be
retired.

The question arises naturally as to whether certain
clauses just happen to be generated in a clause-final position, or whether there is a general prohibition on rules of
extraposition.  We have only seen two purported varieties
of clausal extraposition:  extraposition of comparative and
result clauses, and extraposition of relative clauses.
There have also been purported to be extraposition of noun-
complement clauses (Bill figured a proof out that the circle
could not be squared) and extraposition leaving it (it is
obvious that Jack is a commie).  I cannot replicate any of
the arguments that relative and comparative clauses are
generated in place for these other types.

Furthermore, there is a paradigm discovered by Ross
that provides evidence that there is extraposition of relative and complement clauses from NP that have been wh
Moved to initial position (adapted from Ross (1967:5.1.1.3)).

(100)  a.  Sam picked somebody up who would sleep with him
            before nine.

       b.  Sam picked somebody up before nine who would sleep
            with him.

       c.  *Who did Sam pick up who would sleep with him before
            nine?

       d.  Who did Sam pick up before nine who would sleep
            with him?

(101)  a.  Jane figured six proofs out that the circle could
            not be squared before dawn.

       b.  Jane figured six proofs out before dawn that the
            circle could not be squared.

       c.  *How many proofs did Jane figure out that the circle
            could not be squared before dawn?

       d.  How many proofs did Jane figure out before dawn that
            the circle could not be squared?

Given the assumptions that *wh* Movement puts the preposed
element in COMP, that 'extraposed' relatives and noun complements are generated by a S ──→ S S̄ rule, and that their
heads must be in construction with them at all levels of
the derivation, *(100c) and *(101c) are ruled out as desired.  But (100d) and (101d) should be out as well, and
they are grammatical.  It appears that there actually is a
rule of Extraposition from NP that applies after *wh* Movement, just as proposed by Ross.  Whether this rule applies
to clauses in NP outside of COMP I do not know.

   This analysis requires that it be impossible for split
antecedents of a relative pronoun to be *wh*-Moved, and this
indeed we find to be the case:

(102)  a.  *Who is on the A team and who is on the B team
            who are related?

       b.  *What did you buy and what did you sell that
            were of approximately equal value?

       c.  *What actor married and what actress divorced
            yesterday who once were engaged?

       d.  *Who did you hug and who did you kiss who are
            sisters?

These are the best examples I can find, and, fortunately, they do not quite make the grade.

It is reasonable to ask whether noun phrase complements always extrapose, or whether they can be generated at a distance from their heads. The following example, of a form pointed out to me by Michael Szamosi, shows that complement-like clauses can hang in space next to an idiomatic S:

(103)  The cat is out of the bag that Freebie's on parole.

It thus seems that complement clauses can fill the position created by the S ⟶ S S̄ rule. But (103) is clearly not a noun complement. Should noun complements be generable at a distance from their heads, as are relatives and comparatives, the distinction between the predicate complement system and the determiner complement system would begin to fade, which would be unfortunate (but recall Baltin's example: *the proof which we discussed yesterday that Pi was irrational*).

I now turn to the indefinite comparative. Thiersch (1974) proposed that the subordinate clause originated in the Det of the matrix QP. Taking the *the* in the subordinate clause as its complementizer, he arrives at (104b) as the structure for (104a):

(104)  a.  The more pizza Mary eats, the fatter she gets.

(104) b.

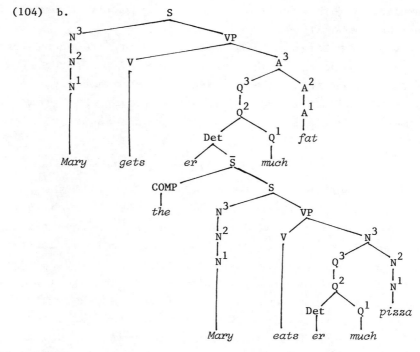

The subordinate clause is then preposed by a rule that replicates the *the*, producing the *the* in the second, matrix,
clause of (104).

We have already seen that these *the's* do not occupy
COMP position, but rather Det position in their associated
QP. Now the fall of the Det source for comparatives makes
this proposal for these constructions considerably less
attractive. Enthusiasm for this wanes still further when
we observe that the *the*-clause preposing would have to be
so constrained as to move the clause to the front of the
clause it had 'scope' over:

(105)   a.  Bill says that the more you study, the less you know.

        b.  The more you study, the less Bill says you know.

By introducing these clauses with the $\bar{S}$ —→ COMP ($\bar{S}$) S ($\bar{S}$)
rule we may subsume them under the generalization noted for
Marathi (section 1.1.3.5) that anticipatory clauses go
semantically on the $\bar{S}$ they're in. In fact one may say
generally that relative and comparative clauses go semantically on the S, if any, that they are sisters with.

Given this proposal, (106) is the deep structure for
(104a):

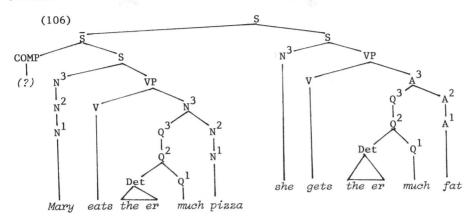

(106)

Observe that preposing of the *the-er* determined constituent happens in both the main and the subordinate
clause.  This suggests that the lexicalists' multi-barrel-
led COMP is really more like the old notion of 'Pre-
Sentence':  a place where all manner of things can be put,
among them complementizers in Bresnan's original sense.

Taking the indefinite comparative as analogous to the
anticipatory relative, we expect to find it in trailing
position as well, and indeed we do:

(107)   a.   You know the less, you more you study.

        b.   Mary gets the fatter, the more pizza she eats.

Observe that in the trailing construction the *the-er* determined constituent does not front.  This structure reinforces
our decision to analyse *the* as part of the Det of QP.

Thiersch observes a construction allied to the trailing
indefinite comparative, in which the matrix does not have a
*the-er* determiner, but an iterated comparative adjective:
*Mary gets fatter and fatter, the more pizzas she eats.*
This construction cannot be anticipatory: *the more pizzas
she eats, the fatter and fatter she gets.*  Thiersch notes
that in this construction the matrix may be uttered by one
speaker and the following clause by another:  *A:  "Mary
gets fatter and fatter".   B: "The more of those pizzas she
eats!"*  The genuine indefinite comparative distinguishes

172

itself from this construction in not being divisible between two speakers in either its trailing or its anticipatory variants: *A: "Mary gets the fatter." B: "The more
pizzas she eats!"; *A: "The more pizzas she eats" B: "The
fatter Mary gets."

I would tentatively conclude that there is in addition
to extraposed and trailing position at the end of the sentence something which I shall call 'afterthought position.'
A clause is essentially independent of its afterthoughts,
which may be uttered by a different speaker or not at all.
Nonrestrictive relatives on sentences in which, but not in
as, have the properties of afterthoughts: as you know, our
funds are being cut, *which you know, our funds are being
cut; *A:"Ivan, our funds are being cut!" I: "as I told you
they would be!", A: "Ivan, our funds are being cut!"
I: "which I already knew!". as thus appears to take the
anticipatory/trailing construction, while which takes the
afterthought construction.

We may finally note for the comparative system a lack
paralleling that pointed out earlier for the relative system: extraposed position is a clause-final position that
for both comparative and relative clauses has a great deal
in common with embedded-headed position. There is no
clause initial position that is related to embedded position.

2.3 Global Relations: I shall now develop the theory of
extra-constituent structure relations that I have frequently invoked in the preceding pages. The theory is a development of interpretive theories of anaphora as explored in
such works as Jackendoff (1972), Wasow (1972), Chomsky
(1973) and Fiengo (1974), and of the 'global grammar' proposed by Lakoff (1971).

There are a number of objections commonly raised against
interpretive theories that I wish to meet in the present
one. The first is "How do you put it together?" Interpretive theories characteristically determine such relations
as coreference or quantifier scope by examination of
various levels of derived structure. How is the information
thus determined integrated with that determined by examina-

tion of other levels of structure so as to form a coherent level of semantic representation? It is commonplace to point out that interpretive theories are really 'global', in the somewhat vague sense in which the word has come to be used. I shall here make fully explicit the nature of the 'globality' involved in my proposals.

Chomsky (1974-75 class lectures) has recently proposed that semantic interpretation is determined from surface structure augmented with 'traces' that mark positions from which things have been moved (see Fiengo (1974) for discussion of traces). Liberman (1974) has shown some interesting things that can be done within such a framework. Should the technical details of this approach prove forthcoming in a satisfactory manner, the provisions I make for globality will be unnecessary. They may, however, be eliminated with no consequences for the structure of the theory. Hence the present developments are compatible both with a traditional interpretivist outlook and with Chomsky's more recent ideas.

A more serious criticism is that interpretive rules are typically made up *ad hoc* for English, coming from no antecendently determined metatheory. There is therefore no clear distinction between the language-particular and the language-universal, and claims to have constrained linguistic theory by depriving the syntax of some power are evacuated by giving a wild card to the rules of interpretation. This charge is not really fair. Jackendoff writes, for example (Jackendoff 1973, p. 380):

> "This is not to say that the rules of semantic interpretation are universal, any more than the base or transformations are. It is clear, for example, that focus and presupposition are not realized with the same syntactic and phonological devices in all languages, and that reflexivization does not universally obey the constraints of English. What is claimed, rather, is that any device used to mark focus and presupposition, be it stress, syntactic position, or a focus morpheme, will be interpreted at the surface structure, conditioning

> a rule which performs the same operations upon the semantic
> interpretation;  whatever the structural conditions on
> reflexivization, if there is reflexivization in a language,
> they will be operative at the end of cycles, conditioning
> a rule making an entry in the table of coreference.  Similarly,
> one might guess that certain aspects of the environment for
> pronominalization and reflexivization are universal;  it might
> turn out that there are only a small number of possible options
> available."

In spite of this, it still must be admitted that interpretive semantics smudges the distinction between language-
particular grammar and universal metatheory outside of the
syntactic component:  there is no serious attempt to distinguish formulations of interpretive rules from the devices that apply them.  Neither can it be said that 'generative semanticists' have done well with the problem.  They
have frequently made assertions that 'global rules' are
better than 'indexing devices', but have not made much
progress on putting satisfactory constraints on either.

In the following pages, I will set up a language-
universal system for imposing certain extra-constituent
structure relations, which I shall call 'global relations',
on the phrase-markers in transformational derivations.
Although most of the details of the system will be determined on the basis of English, the work on relative clauses
in chapter 1 provides some basis for postulating the uni-
versality of the system proposed.  The system will determine the constituent structure relations of relative clauses
and their heads and their relative constituents.  Although
many problems will remain of how languages refer to these
relations in the statement of rules, the result will still
be a more substantially constrained approach to the phenomena than any that I am aware of.  I emphasize again that it
is the fact that the mechanisms are proposed as language
universals that renders them metatheoretical provisions
rather than *ad hoc* descriptions.

There is finally the question raised by McCawley (1973)
of what the objects created by interpretivist rules of

'semantic interpretation' have to do with semantics, as
the term is used by logicians interested in natural language, philosophers of certain persuasions, and, increasingly,
linguists.  I explicitly take the position that the global
relations I postulate are syntactic, rather than semantic,
objects.  They would of course, play a rule in semantic
interpretation:  for example, in systems of the form explored in Cooper and Parsons (1974), where rules are given
for translating constituent structures into logical formu-
lae, the global relations I develop here would tell one
how to assign variables to NP and to variable-binding
operators.  I presume that the contribution of the global
relations to semantic interpretation would be specifiable
universally for natural language.

2.3.1 *Node Indexing*:  Global phenomena (such as the multi-
level semantic interpretation typical of all but the most
recent interpretive theories) require the introduction
into syntax of some scheme of node indexing to keep track
of the 'corresponding nodes' relation. Lakoff (1971) takes
global phenomena as a warrant for sweeping reformulations
in the theory of grammar.  Setting aside the technical difficulties with his proposals (see Soames (1974)), I do not
think that such drastic reformulations are called for.
The phenomena that are solid (and involve matters internal
to the derivation -- the dependencies of derivations on
extra-derivational and even extra-linguistic matters being
a different order of problem) can be dealt with by means of
various localized alterations in the theory, in the style
of Jackendoff.  I shall therefore set up the corresponding
nodes relation so as to make minimum, virtually null,
changes in the theory of grammar.

I shall say that a phrase-marker is a well-formed terminal labelled bracketing in the sense of Peters and Ritchie
(1973) (thereby discarding the original usage of the term
as referring to a set of strings meeting certain conditions
designed to guarantee that it determine a tree).  That is,
a phrase-marker is a string of terminal symbols and labelled brackets in which each bracket matches with a bracket

that has the same label. I furthermore stipulate that in indexed phrase-marker is like a phrase-marker but has the additional feature that each right bracket bears a positive integer as a superscript. Finally, a regularly indexed phrase-marker is an indexed phrase-marker in which the first right bracket has superscript 1, and second 2, and so forth.

It is clear that there is only one way of applying indices to a phrase-marker so as to get a regularly indexed phrase-marker. Therefore, instead of starting out a transformational derivation with a phrase-marker produced by the base, we can start it with the regularly indexed phrase-marker corresponding to one produced by the base (the rules of which could not supply the indices at all without being context sensitive). (108) is then a simplified regularly indexed deep structure for *John admires Mary*:

$$(108) \quad [_S[_{NP}[_N \ John]_N^1]_{NP}^2[_{Aux}[_T \ Pres]_T^3]_{Aux}^4[_{VP}[_V \ admire]_V^5$$
$$[_{NP}[_N \ Mary]_N^6]_{NP}^7]_{VP}^8]_S^9$$

It remains to provide conventions for the preservation of node-indices under transformations.

I believe that the elementaries may be constrained to Deletion, Chomsky adjunction and Substitution. Deletion poses no problem. For the other two, I propose the obvious: the node created by Chomsky adjunction bears the node index (along with all the category features) of the node adjoined to, while in Substitution the node substituted for disappears entirely, along with its index, and is replaced by the substituting node, along with its index. I will give an example involving Substitution.

Bresnan (1972) proposed that passive sentences had underlyingly empty subjects, with the NP in the agent phrase (the logical subject) generated in that position in deep structure. Assuming this, a somewhat simplified deep structure for *John is admired by Mary* might be (109a), with (109b) being the structure derived from (109a) by Object Preposing:

(109) a. $[_S[_{NP}*]^1_{NP}[_{Aux}[_T Pres]^2_T]^3_{Aux}[_{VP}[_{Pass} be\ en]^4_{Pass}$

$[_V admire]^5_V[_{NP}[_N Mary]^6_N]^7_{NP}[_{PP}[_P by]^8_P$

$[_{NP}[_N John]^9_N]^{10}_{NP}]^{11}_{PP}]^{12}_{VP}]^{13}_S$

b. $[_S[_{NP}[_N Mary]^6_N]^7_{NP}[_{Aux}[_T Pres]^2_T]^3_{Aux}[_{VP}[_{Pass} be\ en$

$]^4_{Pass}[_V admire]^5_V[_{PP}[_P by]^8_P[_{NP}[_N John]^9_N]^{10}_{NP}]^{11}_{PP}$

$]^{12}_{VP}]^{13}_S$

'*' is a special terminal hypothesized by Fiengo (1974) to be insertable by convention under any phrase node in the base. A derivation that reaches the surface with surviving '*' is ungrammatical. Hence Object preposing must apply to (109a), there being no other applicable rule that could erase the '*' (Fiengo supposes that there is a rule of agent postposing that applies in Passives, putting the subject into the *-filled NP of a *by*-phrase, but this is an independent matter).

Fiengo also proposes that when a constituent is moved, the symbol 't' is left in the position from which the constituent is extracted. 't' is said to be 'bound' by the moved constituent, and if a derivation reaches the surface with a 't' (trace) which commands and precedes that which binds it, then the derivation blocks. Agent postposing thus may yield a structure exactly like (109a) with '*' replaced by 't', to which Object preposing must apply to erase the trace.

We might formalise Fiengo's proposal by recasting the deletion elementary so as to replace each maximal deleted constituent with $'[_L t]^n_L'$ where L is the label of that constituent and $n$ is its index. Carrying this out in a framework in which variables are deleted is rather messy. In Fiengo's framework, the Deletion elementary is restricted to constituents, and furthermore to constituents which the transformation doing the deletion replicates elsewhere by Substitution or Chomsky adjunction.

With traces left by movement in the manner specified

above, Object preposing would derive (110) from (109a):

(110)   $[_S[_{NP}[_N \ Mary]_N^6]_{NP}^7[_{Aux}[_T \ Pres]_T^2]_{Aux}^3[_{VP}[_{Pass} \ be \ en$
$]_{Pass}^4[_V \ admire]_V^5[_{NP}t]_{NP}^7[_{PP}[_P \ by]_P^8[_{NP}[_N \ John$
$]_N^9]_{NP}^{10}]_{PP}^{11}]_{VP}^{12}]_S^{13}$

There is a final problem connected with the rule of Right Node Raising and other potential rules applying to coordinate structures. Some of these rules perhaps have the effect of fusing two constituents into one. What relation does the index of *John* in *Bill admires, and Susan detests, John* have to do with the indices of the two occurrences of *John* in *Bill admires John and Susan detests John*? It is not clear to me what sort of operations effect Right Node Raising, so any decision here is somewhat premature, but I will venture the guess that it is the final node of the last conjunct that is raised, with the final nodes of the others being deleted. Hence the raised *John* will have the index of the underlying second occurrence of *John*.

If we now associate with a constituent structure a relation specified in the form of some sort of table composed of node-indices, we can apply transformations to the constituent structure, and the table will continue to induce the relations we desire over the constituent structures derived by the transformations. We can thus represent those properties and relations which seem to be globally present in the derivation without any significant disruption in the theory of grammar.

One might in fact claim that a node-indexing scheme was implicit in the *Aspects* theory of grammar, and even in that of *Syntactic Structures*. For in the *Aspects* framework the structural description of a sentence is a pair (∅,   ), where ∅ is a surface structure and   is its deep structure. One of the tasks of the structural description is to indicate the underlying grammatical relations between the constituents of the surface structure.   It is difficult to imagine how the structural description could accomplish this without the aid of a node-indexing scheme.

I will illustrate the technique with an over-simplified

treatment of coreference. Generate a regularly indexed
deep structure, take it to surface structure with the transformational component, and then set up a table of coreference as a set of ordered pairs of node-indices meeting the
following conditions:

(111) a. each index that appears in the table indexes an
NP node in the surface structure

b. the table determines an equivalence relation

c. if $(x, y)$ is in the table, and the node indexed
by $x$ precedes and commands the node indexed by
$y$, then the node indexed by $y$ is a pronoun

Condition (111c) is derived from unpublished work by Howard
Lasnik. A well-formed sentence structure is then a triple
$(\Phi, \psi, C)$, where $\psi$ is a regularly indexed deep structure
provided by the base, $\Phi$ is derived from $\psi$ by the transformational component, and $C$ is a table of coreference assigned
to $\psi$ by (111). The sentence structure can clearly determine a semantic interpretation in the desired manner.

The treatment above is of course only illustrative:
it does not treat of reflexivization, for example. But the
technique is obviously applicable to more sophisticated proposals, such as those of Jackendoff (1972).

There is no essential difference between this kind of
treatment and one in which the relevant properties and
relations are inscribed directly into the phrase-markers,
as by the 'coreference index' proposal of *Aspects*. I
believe, however, that the present approach is somewhat more
perspicuous to the mind.

It is obvious that we must specify exactly what sorts
of tables are allowed in universal grammar, and how they
may be tied to syntactic structure. Without such specifications, a mechanism such as the one I have proposed is
merely an arbitrary indexing device, allowing such absurd
consequences as those pointed out by Cole (1973).

2.3.2 *The Head-COMP Relation*: We have seen various reasons
for believing that there is some sort of relation subsisting
between a relative or comparative clause and its head.

There is first of all the fact that these clauses have their heads in construction with them, even though they may be separated by an unbounded stretch of material. Next, we may observe the *er...than.../as...as...* dependencies and the mirror-image constraint in the English comparative system, or the requirement in the Indic languages discussed in chapter 1 that the head of an anticipatory relative be definite. We may also observe such paradigms as (112) (based on Vergnaud (1974:90-93):

(112)  a.  The woman started sewing and the man started reading who had been shouting at each other.

        b.  A woman started sewing and a man started reading who had been shouting at each other.

        c.  *The woman started sewing and a man started reading who had been shouting at each other.

        d.  *A woman started sewing and the man started reading who had been shouting at each other.

Something has to squeeze these determiners into a ball in order to enforce the requirement that they be the same.

There are essentially two ways in which one might go about setting up such a system. We might say that there was a direct relation subsisting between the head and its 'equivalent' constituent in the dependent clause. We may represent this situation with the diagram (113):

(113)   ...A...[$_{\bar{S}}$ COMP...B...]...

The $\bar{S}$ that is the relative or comparative clause (and thereby its COMP) is uniquely identified because it is the maximal constituent dominating the 'target' (dependent) constituent but not the head.

Unfortunately, many of the properties of comparatives are replicated by result clauses and infinitive complements of *too*; *so...that...* and *too...for...* present the same selection problem as to *er...than...* and *as...as...* . We may furthermore see that these constructions also obey the mirror-image constraint:

(114)  a.  So many more people than I invited that I couldn't count them came to the party.

b. *So many more people that I couldn't count them than
I invited came to the party.

c. So many more people than I invited came to the party
that I couldn't count them.

d. *So many more people that I couldn't count them came
to the party than I invited.

e. So many more people came to the party than I invited
that I couldn't count them.

f. *So many more people came to the party that I couldn't
count them than I invited.

(115) a. Too many more people than I invited for us to count
came to the party.

b. *Too many more people for us to count than I invited
came to the party.

c. Too many more people than I invited came to the
party for us to count.

d. *Too many more people for us to count came to the
party than I invited.

e. Too many more people came to the party than I
invited for us to count.

f. *Too many more people came to the party for us
to count than I invited.

We therefore need a relation that holds between the clause
and its head.

Since the morphology of the COMP and the morphology of
the Det of the head are interdependent, I will represent
the relation as holding between the Det of the head and
the COMP of the clause, and call the relation the Head-
COMP relation.

Questions with *wh*-words are in many ways analogous to
relative clauses. But since questions lack heads, we
could not use a head-target constituent relation to identify the target constituents of a question in the fashion
of (113). Rather, there must be a relation (usually forma-
lized as co-indexing) between the COMP of the question and
its target constituent. Let this relation be called the
COMP-target relationship. If we assume that it subsists
in relative clauses as well as in interrogatives, we may

replace (113) with (116):

(116)   ...A...[$_{\bar{S}}$ COMP...B...]...

(113) and (116) are pretty much the most economical way to represent the necessary relations for relative and comparative clauses, and when we look at more clause types, (116) turns out to require the fewest sorts of primitive relations.  In this subsection, I will develop the axioms for the Head-COMP relation, and in the next those for the COMP-target relation.

We have seen that a COMP can have a whole set of heads. Hence we want the Head-COMP table (referred to henceforth as $H$) to consist of a set of $n$-tuples $(x, y_1, \ldots, y_n)$ where $x$ is the index of a COMP node and $y_1, \ldots, y_n$ are the indices of Det nodes.  We will want an axiom to enforce the requirement that the heads are in construction with, but not contained by, the $\bar{S}$ of the COMP.  This is achieved by (117b) below.  We may secondly observe that a Det can be head for only one COMP, and I will also suppose that for each COMP there is only one entry.  This is accomplished by (117c).  I thus give the following principles governing the assignment of a Head-COMP table to an indexed phrase-marker:

(117)   For an indexed phrase-marker $\phi$, $H$ is a well-formed
         Head-COMP table only if

$$H = \left\{ (x_1, y_{1,1}, \ldots, y_{1,m_1}), \right.$$
$$\vdots$$
$$\left. (x_n, y_{n,1}, \ldots, y_{n,m_n}) \right\}$$

where

(a)   for $i = 1, \ldots, n$, $x_i$ is the index of a COMP
       in $\phi$ and for $j = 1, \ldots, m_j$, $y_{i,j}$
       is the index of a Det in $\phi$.

(b) if $(x, y_1, \ldots, y_m) \, \varepsilon \, H$, then the nodes
indexed by $y_1, \ldots, y_m$ are not dominated by
the node immediately dominating the node
indexed by $x$, but they are dominated by
the node immediately dominating that node.

(c) $H$ mentions no index twice.

(117) captures the major structural conditions. To actually
rule sentences out, however, we need an additional mechanism to enforce some requirements of consistency.

Edmonds (1970), Chomsky (1973) and Vergnaud (1974) have
proposed analyses in which COMP is treated as an increasingly complex node, expanding into a wide variety of things.
I shall develop this further by supposing that there is a
'place' in COMP wherein are placed the features of the
determiners that the COMP may take as head. Whether this
'place' should be treated as a constituent or as a new kind
of feature I do not really know. I shall take the latter
course. I shall represent it as a symbol $[\pm F_1 \ldots \pm F_k]_D$,
where the $\pm F_i$ are the features over which consistency is
enforced. This symbol may be treated as a component of the
label of the COMP brackets. By requiring the $[\ldots]_D$ symbol
to be featurally nondistinct from those of the determiners
of the heads, we require these determiners to all have the
same composition, and furthermore permit that composition
to determine the formative used to spell the COMP. This
solves the problem of the *er...than.../as...as...* selection-
al dependencies.

We may also observe that some clauses, such as English
comparatives, or ordinary English relatives, require heads,
while others, such as ordinary Navajo relatives, do not.
We thus may suppose that there is in COMP a universal
feature [±Hd]. A COMP that is [+Hd] must have a head; one
that is [-Hd] does not have a head. I propose that the
$[\ldots]_D$ symbol is present regardless of whether or not there
is a head.

Formally, we may capture these requirements as follows:

(118)  If $\phi$ is a phrase marker, and $H$ is a well formed
       Head-COMP table for $\phi$, then
       (a) if $x$ is the index of a [+COMP +Hd] node
           in  , then there are $y_1$, ..., $y_m$ such
           that $(x, y_1, ..., y_m)$ is an element of $H$
       (b) if $(x, y_1, ..., y_m)$ is an element of $H$
           then the node indexed by $x$ is
           [+Hd $[...]_D$], where '[...]' is non-
           distinct from the node indexed by
           each $y_i$, $i = 1$, ..., $m$.

Finally, we must propose a feature system. I shall first
distinguish nominal determiners from QP determiners by
having the former be [+ND −QD] and the latter [−ND +QD].
Amongst the nominal determiners, *the* is of course [+Def]
while *a*, etc., is [−Def]. Amongst the QP determiners *er*
and *as* will be [+Cm −Rs] and *too* and *so* will be [−Cm +Rs].
(Cm for 'comparative', Rs for 'resultative'). Finally, *er*
will be [+≠], and *as* will be [−≠], while *too* will be [+Ex]
and *so* will be [−Ex]. My choices here are somewhat arbitrary, serving merely to distinguish from each other the
formatives involved, and to impose upon them an intuitively
reasonable classification. At present, I would not suppose
that these features are at all the correct ones. I do
believe, however, that the correct features should be taken
as belonging to some language-universal feature framework.
Much more work in various languages would be required to
acquire a real understanding of the kind of feature system
necessary.

We can now see that we need merely specify that *than*
goes into a [+COMP +Hd [−ND +QD +Cm +Rs + ≠]$_D$] node in
order to state the fundamental facts of its distribution.
The other complementizers may be dealt with in a precisely
comparable fashion. The feature +R introduced in Chapter 1
to distinguish the complementizers of relative clauses may
be taken to be a symbol for [+ND −QD ...]$_D$.

We are now in a position to rule out some sentences.
I shall first consider an example in which a comparative
clause occurs in an S together with a QP that has the

appropriate determiner, but the clause is not in construction with the QP:

(119)

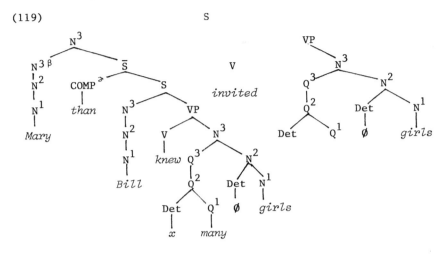

I have left out various inessential nodes, and given only
certain crucial node-indices in the form of Greek-letter
superscripts.

By the lexicon, ∂ must be [+COMP +Hd]. But then, by
(118a), there must be $(x, y_1, \ldots, y_n) \varepsilon H$ such that $x = \partial$,
and by (117a) the nodes indexed by $y_1, \ldots, y_n$ must be
[+Det]. But by (117b), they must be in β, and there are
no such nodes in β. Therefore the structure has no Head-
COMP table that satisfies the required conditions, and the
sentence *Mary [than Bill know girls] invited more girls is
ruled out. QED.

Another example, in which the constituent structures
are O.K. but the determiners and complementizers do not
agree properly, is (120):

186

(120)

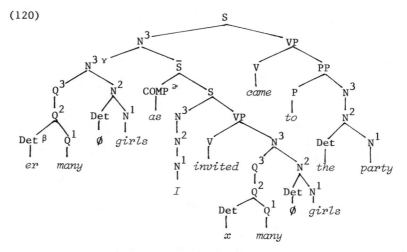

By the lexicon, *ə* will be [+COMP +Hd [−ND +QD +Cm −Rs −≠]$_D$].
But by (118a), there must be (*ə*, $y_1$, ..., $y_m$) ε *H*, where
$y_1$, ..., $y_m$ index determiners within ɣ.   β is the only
candidate.  But β is [−ND +QD +Cm −Rs +≠], so it disagrees
with ɣ, and therefore condition (118b) cannot be met.
Hence the sentence *more girls as I invited came to the
party* has no well formed Head-COMP table and is therefore
ungrammatical.

Now let us consider the mirror-image constraint.  (121)
is a typical acceptable structure and (122) is a typical
violation:

(121)  *As* many *er* many people *than* I invited *as* you

predicted came to the party.

(122)  **As* many *er* many people *as* you predicted *than* I

invited came to the party.

There are sufficiently many other string-tangling phenomena
in syntax to make a formulation of the constraint premature
(or trivial).  I merely observe that the Head-COMP relation
provides the strings to tangle.

Multiple headed comparatives and result clauses are
compatible with the principles (117-118).  They enforce the
requirement that the determiners all be the same. That this

is correct is evidenced by (123):

(123) a. Fewer people moved more cinder blocks this time
than ever before.

b. As many people moved as many cinder blocks this
time as ever before.

c. *As many people moved more cinder blocks this
time as/than ever before.

Note the inexplicable *as few people moved as many cinder
blocks this time as ever before. This somewhat casts into
doubt the significance of (123).

More interesting cases of the consistency requirement
being enforced are those involving relatives, since here,
there is no overt formative in the COMP that is selected on
the basis of what appears in the determiners of the head.
Relative clauses also give some evidence with regard to
what features the consistency requirement is to be enforced
over. (124) is grammatical:

(124) One man came in and three women went out who
were related.

Yet the Det of one man is [+Sg] and that of three women is
[-Sg]. This shows that ±Sg is not specified in $[...]_D$.

This leads to an immediate prediction: because ±Def
appears in $[...]_D$, there will be languages in which there
are complementizers that require definite heads, and
because ±Sg is not in $[...]_D$ there will not be languages
in which there are complementizers that require singular
heads. As far as I know, both of these predictions are
borne out. In Navajo (sections 1.1.2.1, 1.1.3.6), the
complementizer ígíí/ęę is only used to form definite descriptions, whether in the internal head, pre-relative or
extraposed relative construction. We may thus specify
ígíí/ęę in the lexicon as being [+COMP [+ND −QD +Def]$_D$]
leaving it unspecified with respect to ±Hd (the features
that specifies whether there is a head or not). English
contains a near miss to the claim that no languages have
complementizers that select a certain number on their heads
in the form of the paucal relative clause (section 1.1.2.2).

The reader may well be suspicious about one of the properties of (117): (117a) involves a crucial mention of the category 'Det'. Our suspicions deepen when we note that there are words such as *sufficient/sufficiently*, that are clearly A, and *enough*, which the *$Q^0$ $A^0$ Filter shows to be a Q (*tall enough*, *\*enough tall*; *different enough*, *enough different*), that take *for* (and maybe sometimes *that*) complements, just as does *too*.

Reflecting on this problem leads us to an important revision in (117-118). Why not say that the COMP is connected not to a Det, but to a [-COMP] node bearing a $[...]_D$ feature.[7] The consistency requirement is then merely that the contents of the two $[...]_D$ features be identical (or perhaps nondistinct).

Making this move, we can form a unified reformulation of (117, 118), combining (117a) and (118b):

(125)  For an indexed phrase-marker $\phi$, $H$ is a well-formed
       Head-COMP table only if
       $$H = (x_1, y_{1,1}, \ldots, y_{1,m_1}),$$

       $$(x_n, y_{n,1}, \ldots, y_{n,m_n})$$
       where

(a) for $i = 1, \ldots, n$, $x_i$ is the index of a
    [+COMP +Hd $[...]_D$]node in $\phi$ and for $1 \leqslant j \leqslant m_i$,
    $y_{i,j}$ is the index of a [-COMP $[---]_D$]
    node such that ... is identical to ---

(b) if $(x, y_1, \ldots, y_m) \, \varepsilon \, H$, then the nodes
    indexed by $y_1, \ldots, y_m$ are not dominated
    by the node immediately dominating the
    node indexed by $x$, but they are dominated
    by the node immediately dominating that node

(c) no index is mentioned twice in $H$

    (e)  if $x$ is the index of a [+COMP +Hd] node

          in $\phi$, then there are $y_1, \ldots, y_m$ such

          that $(x, y_1, \ldots, y_m) \; \varepsilon \; H$

We may classify a node that is a $[\ldots]_D$ symbol as [+D],
and one that lacks one as [-D]. [+D] is then the feature
borne by those elements that participate in the determiner
complement system, be they determiners or not. 'D' may be
thought of as something that is either absent, or present
in a variety of forms (but not, of course, being absent in
a variety of forms).

    At what level of the derivation does (125) hold? one
possibility is that it holds only at surface structure. In
this case, our elimination of the 'Det' specification was
well advised, for *er* Shift surely removes the Det node from
over *er*. Under our new treatment, however, it need only be
assured that *er* Shift moves the $[\ldots]_D$ specification onto
the Q: *more* can then be treated like *enough*.

    If semantic interpretation can be determined entirely
off of surface structure, then we can effect a grand sim-
plification of the theory by simply eliminating the indices,
and building $H$ out of occurrences of substrings in the
labelled bracketing that is the surface structure. There
is another interesting possibility, however, which is to
claim that (125) holds for $H$ throughout a derivation. One
would generate an indexed deep structure, supply a Head-
COMP table, check to see if (125) was satisfied, and then
in the derivation recheck after each rule has applied. (125)
would then serve to prohibit a wide variety of derivational
shenanigans.

    I have sought to explain some phenomena by means of the
hypothesis that there is in COMP something, I shall call it
a complex feature, that recapitulates the determiner of the
head, or, more accurately, the determiner-like aspect of
the head. When there is no head, this complex feature
performs the function that the head's determiner would
perform. We are saying, then, that it is in some sense
essential for the relative clause to have a determiner, and
that it is the same as the determiner of the head, if there

is any. This is not a new idea in linguistics, being one of the central proposals in Benveniste's classic (1975) article on the relative clause.

2.3.3 *The COMP-Target Relation:* To complete the picture, it remains to set up the relation that holds between COMP and the target constituents. This relation can be set up as a table $T$ of sequences, similar to $H$, the head-COMP table, but obeying somewhat different conditions. From the existence of multiple *wh* word questions and relative clauses, we can see the necessity for a COMP to have several targets. But clearly, a target is related to only one COMP. There is the further requirement that the target(s) be contained within the $\bar{S}$ of the COMP.

These principles may be given a preliminary form as (125):

(126)  For an indexed phrase marker $\phi$, $T$ is a well-formed COMP-Target table only if

$$T = (x_1, y_{1,1}, \ldots, y_{1, m_1}),$$
$$\vdots$$
$$(x_n, y_{n,1}, \ldots, y_{n,m_n})$$

where

(a)  for $i = 1, \ldots, n$, $x_n$ indexes a COMP in $\phi$

for $j = 1, \ldots, n_m$, $y_{i,j}$ indexes a Det in $\phi$

(b)  If $(x, y_1, \ldots, y_m) \; \varepsilon \; T$, then the node immediately dominating the node indexed by $x$ dominates the nodes indexed by $y_1, \ldots, y_m$

(c)  no index is mentioned twice in $T$.

(126) is obviously parallel to (117).

(126) is by itself insufficient. We need something comparable to (118) to permit the lexical entries of formatives to specify that the formative is a relative pronoun, an interrogative, or whatever. We find, furthermore, something analogous to a consistency requirement: in the great

majority of languages, the relative pronoun is different in form from the interrogative. Hence the relative/interrogative pronoun choice is varying with the R/Q choice in the complementizer. I thus posit a complex feature 'W', which may contain the specification '+Q' for 'interrogative', and '-Q' for relative. A relative complementizer will have the feature composition $[+COMP\ [-Q]_W]$, an interrogative complementizer (for a $wh$ word question) will have the composition $[+COMP\ [+Q]_W]$, a relative pronoun will be $[-COMP\ [-Q]_W]$ and an interrogative will be $[-COMP\ [+Q]_W]$.

We can thus formulate (127), parallel to (125):

(127)   For an indexed phrase marker $\phi$, $T$ is a well-

formed COMP-Target table only if

$$T = (x_1,\ y_{1,1},\ \ldots,\ y_{1,m_1}),$$
$$\cdot$$
$$\cdot$$
$$\cdot$$
$$(x_n,\ y_{n,1},\ \ldots,\ y_{n,m_n})$$

where

(a)   for $i = 1,\ \ldots,\ n$, $x_n$ indexes a $[+COMP\ [\ldots]_W]$

node and for $j = 1,\ \ldots,\ m_n$, $y_{i,j}$

indexes a $[-COMP\ [---]_W]$ node such that

$\ldots$ is the same as $---$.

(b)   If $(x,\ y_1,\ \ldots,\ y_m)\ \epsilon\ T$, then for $i =$

$1,\ \ldots,\ m$, the node immediately dominating

the node indexed by $x$ dominates the node

indexed by $y_i$.

(c)   no index is mentioned twice in $T$

(d)   If $z$ indexes a node that is $[[\ldots]_W]$,

then there are $x,\ y_1,\ \ldots,\ y_m$ such

that $(x,\ y_1,\ \ldots,\ y_m)\ \epsilon\ T$ and either

$z = x$ or for some $i$, $1 \leqslant i \leqslant m$, $z = y_i$.

I leave open the full range of contents of the $[...]_W$ complex feature.

We can now specify the features we have used in the lexical entries for various pronouns so as to characterize their uses. English *wh*, for example, is [-COMP +W]. Modern Greek *o opíos* (a relative pronoun that cannot be used as an interrogative) is $[-COMP [-Q]_W]$.

We may deal with multiple headed constructions on the basis of the observation that multiple headed relative clauses either have several antecedents for one relative pronoun, or one antecedent for each relative pronoun. We do not find analogues to the teratologism (128):

(128)   *A man$_i$ killed a woman$_j$ and a boy$_h$ kissed a girl$_k$

which males$_{i,h}$ were in love with which$_{j,k}$ females.

The following principle may therefore be proposed:

(129)   If $\phi$ is an indexed phrase marker with Head–COMP
table $H$ and COMP–Target table $T$, then if
$(x, y_1, ..., y_n)$ ε $H$ and $x, z_1, ..., z_m)$ ε $T$
either $m = 1$ or $m = n$.

(129) enforces the restriction that in a relative clause with several *wh* words, each has its own head.

There are many ways in which one could continue to tighten up the system so as to capture well-known constraints. The 'strong crossover principle' that Crow (section 1.2.1.1) reveals to apply to *wh*-marking is an obvious candidate, and so is Chomsky's (1973) constraint that a *wh* word that is in a COMP is interpreted as bound by that COMP. I shall restrict myself to getting the system to recognize the major constituent structure types.

We may clearly discern three important kinds of relative clauses: the anticipatory and trailing relatives, the pre-, post- and extraposed relatives, and the headless relatives. I shall assume here that the pre- and post-relatives are all underlyingly what they are on the surface, hence rejecting the extraction analysis. (Observe that under the extraction analysis, the situation would arise in which the surface structure head and NP$_{rel}$ would have the same node index: thus the various *the's* in the well-formedness relations for the tables would suffer from presupposition failure. I can see no problem in replacing all these *the's* with *a*'s). Comparative clauses fall into the first two families. I shall call the first family the adjoined clauses, the second the headed embedded, and the last the headless, as suggested in section 1.1.3.

We wish to explain the fact that typically, *wh* words and complementizers are usable in one, but not all of the three types of clauses. We further see in the indefinite comparative reason to believe that $NP_{rel}$ and $NP_{hd}$ share some complex feature.

I shall suppose that $NP_{rel}$ shares the $[\ldots]_D$ feature of its controlling COMP. This may be enforced by the following stipulation:

(130)  If $\phi$ is a phrase marker with a well-formed COMP-Target relation $T$, and if for $(x, y_1, \ldots, y_m)$ $\varepsilon$ $T$ and for $i = 1, \ldots, m$, then the node indexed by $x$ agrees with the node indexed by $y_i$ on the composition of $[\ldots]_D$.

I then suppose the various positional environments to impose a feature on the $[\ldots]_D$ of the COMP of the relative clause. By (130), these specifications are also enforced in $NP_{rel}$ and $NP_{hd}$, and so can influence the form of determiners, etc.

The three families may be distinguished with the features ±Ad and ±At. Anticipatory and trailing relatives are [+Ad -At]. Clauses generated by a rule of the form $X \rightarrow X \bar{S}$ or $X \rightarrow \bar{S} X$ are [-Ad +At]. Finally, clauses generated by $X \rightarrow \bar{S}$ (headless clauses) are [-Ad -At]. Putting this in symbols, we get (131):

(131)  If a $[+COMP [-Q]_W]$node is immediately dominated by
   (a)  an $\bar{S}$ immediately dominated by $\bar{S}$, then it is also $[[+Ad -At]_D]$.
   (b)  an $\bar{S}$ immediately dominated by an X and sister to an X (where X is a category variable), then it is also $[[-Ad +At]_D]$

(c) an $\bar{S}$ immediately dominated by X and sister
     to nothing, then it is also $[[-Ad -At]_D]$.

We may now distinguish some words by their featural specifications. Relative *which* is specified as $[-COMP [-Q]_W$
$[+ND -QD -Ad +A]_D]$. *the er* is $[-COMP [-ND +QD +Ad -At]_D]$.
Bresnan's 'x' determiner is $[-COMP [-Q]_W [-ND +QD -Ad +At]_D]$.

Before closing the section and the chapter, I will describe briefly some principles that would assist a language
learner in sorting out these types on the basis of minimal
evidence. First, consider the extraposed versus the
trailing clauses. Trailing clauses characteristically can
appear in anticipatory position, but there is no matrix
initial position for extraposed clauses. Note that this is
also the case for afterthought clauses. If we suppose that
intonation patterns suffice to distinguish afterthought
from extraposed clauses, then we can discern the trailing
clauses to be the non-afterthought clauses that never
appear matrix initially. I suspect that intonation would
also serve to distinguish extraposed from trailing clauses,
which suggests that these positional facts are not really
relevant to language-learning.

We have also observed a general principle that in a
clause introduced by an X → X $\bar{S}$ or S → $\bar{S}$ X rule, which I
shall also call an attached relative, $NP_{rel}$ must usually be
a pronoun, with Japanese being an apparent exception to
this. We may establish a principle that includes Japanese
under a non-extraction analysis (see section 1.3.1) by
stipulating that in an attached relative structure $NP_{rel}$ be
anaphoric to $NP_{hd}$ in the sense of Wasow (1972). It is a
basic principle of anaphora that if NP A is anaphoric to
NP B, then A must be more general than B. In the typical
anticipatory relative, $NP_{rel}$ is less general (i.e., is an
NP like *wh-horse*), while $NP_{hd}$ is just a pronoun. Hence
the typical anticipatory relative cannot be misanalysed
as a pre-relative without leading to violations of universal conditions.

There is a final consequence that we can extract from
the anaphoricity condition. Vergnaud (1974) observes a

constraint that a pronoun cannot be anaphoric to a containing NP. Hence (132) are ungrammatical:

(132)  a.  *The fact$_i$ that it$_i$ was discovered is amazing.

b.  *Pictures$_i$ of collectors of them$_i$ are on the wall.

This condition, together with the condition that NP$_{rel}$ of an attached relative clauses be anaphoric to NP$_{hd}$ requires that an embedded relative attached to an NP be introduced by NP → NP $\bar{S}$:  for NOM → NOM $\bar{S}$, and N → N $\bar{S}$ would not provide for NP$_{rel}$ an NP$_{hd}$ that did not dominate it.  Hence solely on the basis of examples like *the boy who died*, etc., we are forced to get the NP → NP $\bar{S}$ rule, which provides the constituent structure needed for the examples like *the boy and the girl who were engaged*.

The system of relations would thus appear to permit one to formulate principles that contribute in a demonstrable way towards making relative clause construction in principle learnable.

## FOOTNOTES TO CHAPTER 2

1.    Much of the material in this chapter is based on this
article, which I shall henceforth refer to as merely
'Bresnan'.   I am heavily indebted to Joan Bresnan and Mark
Liberman for discussions of many of the subjects treated
here.
2.    I am indebted to Dorothy Siegel for uttering this
example, and to Mark Liberman for pointing out that she had.

# BIBLIOGRAPHY

Anderson, S.R: in preparation, 'Ergativity and Linguistic Structure.'

Anderson, S.R. and P. Kiparksy, (eds.): 1973, A Festschrift for Morris Halle, Holt, Rinehart and Winston.

Andrews, A.D.: 1974, 'One(s) Deletion in the Comparative Clause,' in NELS V, 246-255.

Ashton, E.O.: 1944, Swahili Grammar, London: Green & Co..

Bach. Emmon: 1965, 'On Some Recurrent Types of Transformations,' in C. W. Kreidler (ed.), Sixteenth Annual Round Table Meeting on Linguistics and Language Studies, Georgetown University Monograph Series on Languages and Linguistics 18.

Baker, C.L.: 1965, Indirect Questions in English, unpublished Ph.D. dissertation, Indiana University.

Baker, C.L.: 1970, 'Notes on the Description of English Questions: the Role of an Abstract Question Morpheme,' Foundations of Language 6, 197-219.

Benveniste, Émile: 1957, 'La Phrase Relative, Problème de Syntax Générale,' in Problèmes de Linguistique Générale, Paris: Galimard.

Bergsland, Knut: 1965, 'A Grammatical Outline of the Eskimo Language of West Greenland,' ms., Oslo.

Bowers, John: 1970, 'Adjectives and Adverbs in English,' distributed by the Indiana University Linguistics Club.

Brame, M.K.: 1968, 'A New Analysis of the Relative Clause: Evidence for an Interpretive Theory,' ms., MIT.

Bresnan, J.W.: 1970, 'On Complementizers: Towards a Syntactic Theory of Complement Types,' Foundations of Language 6, 297-321.

Bresnan, J.W.: 1972, The Theory of Complementation in English Syntax, unpublished Ph.D. dissertation, MIT.

Bresnan, J.W.: 1973, 'Syntax of the Comparative Clause Construction in English,' Linguistic Inquiry 4, 275-344.

Bresnan, J.W.: 1974a, 'On the Position of Certain Clause Particles in Phrase Structure,' Linguistic Inquiry 5, 614-619.

Bresnan, J.W.: 1974b, 'Comparative Deletion and Constraints on Transformations,' Linguistic Analysis 1, 25-74. Actually appeared in 1975.

Browne, Wayles: 1970, 'More on Definite Markers: Interrogatives in Persian,' Linguistic Inquiry 1, 259-263.

Carslon, G.N. and L.W. Martin: 1974, 'Relative Clauses and Resumptive Pronouns,' ms., University of Iowa.

Chomsky, N.A.: 1957, Syntactic Structures, The Hague: Mouton.

Chomsky, N.A.: 1965, Aspects of the Theory of Syntax, Cambridge, MA: MIT Press.

Chomsky, N.A.: 1970, 'Remarks on Nominalization,' in Peters and Rosenbaum (eds.).

Chomksy, N.A.: 1973, 'Conditions on Transformations,' in Anderson and Kiparsky (eds.).

Cooper, Robin and Terence Parsons: 1974, 'Montague Grammar, Generative Semantics and Interpretive Semantics,' published in Partee, B.H. (ed.) (1976), Montague Grammar, Academic Press.

Cole, Peter: 1973, 'Global Grammar and Index Grammar,' Studies in the Linguistic Sciences 3:1, University of Illinois.

Donaldson, Susan: 1971, 'Movement in Restrictive Relative Clauses in Hindi,' Studies in the Linguistic Sciences 1:2, University of Illinois.

East African Swahili Committee: 1955-58, Studies in Swahili Dialect, Kampala: Maberere College.

Emonds, J.E.: 1970, Root and Structure Preserving Transformations, unpublished Ph.D. dissertation, MIT. Distributed by the Indiana University Linguistics Club. Revised version published in 1976 as A Transformational Approach to English Syntax, Academic Press.

Fiengo, R.W.: 1974, Semantic Conditions on Surface Structure, unpublished Ph.D. dissertation, MIT. Revised version published in 1980 as Surface Structure: the Intersection of Autonomous Components, Harvard University Press.

Geis, M.L.: 1970, Adverbial Subordinate Clauses in English, unpublished Ph.D. dissertation, MIT.

Ginsburg, Seymour and Parbara Partee: 1969, 'A Mathematical Model for Transformational Grammars,' Information and Control 16, 297-334.

Gorbet, L.F.: 1974, Relativization and Complementation in Diegueno: Noun Phrases as Nouns, unpublished Ph.D. dissertation, UCSD.

Hale, K.H.: 1970, 'Relative Clauses in Some Non-Indo-European Languages,' Paper presented at NELS V, Cambridge, MA. Warlpiri data published in Hale (1976).

Hale, K.H.: 1976, 'The Adjoined Relative Clause in Australia,' in R.M.W. Dixon (ed.), Grammatical Categories in Australian Languages, Canberra: Australian Institute of Aboriginal Studies.

Hankamer, Jorge: 1971, Constraints on Deletion in Syntax, unpublished Ph.D. dissertation, Yale University. Published in 1979 by Garland Press.

Hankamer, Jorge: 1974, 'On Wh Indexing,' in NELS V, 61-76.

Hintikka, Jaakko: 1974, 'Quantifiers vs. Quantification Theory,' Linguistic Inquiry 5, 153-178.

Jackendoff, R.S.: 1972, Semantic Interpretation in Generative Grammar, Cambridge, MA: MIT Press.

Jackendoff, R.S.: 1973, 'The Base Rules for Prepositions,' in Anderson and Kiparsky (eds.).

Jacobs, Roderick, and Peter Rosenbaum, (eds.): 1970, Readings In English Transformational Grammar, Waltham, MA: Ginn and Co..

Jeanne, Laverne: 1974, 'The Relative Clause in Hopi,' ms., MIT.

Junghare, I.Y.: undated, 'Restrictive Relative Clauses in Marathi,' ms., University of Minnesota.

Kaufman, E.S.: 1974, 'Navajo Spatial Enclitics: A Case for Unbounded Movement,' Linguistic Inquiry 5, 507-534.

Keenan, E.L.: 1972, 'On Semantically Based Grammar,' Linguistic Inquiry 3, 412-462.

Keenan, E.L. and Bernard Comrie: 1972, 'NP Accessibility and Universal Grammar,' ms.. Published as Keenan and Comrie (1977).

Keenan, E.L. and Bernard Comrie: 1977, 'Noun Phrase Accessiblity and Universal Grammar,' Linguistic Inquiry 8, 63-99.

Kleinschmidt, S.: 1851, Grammatik der Grönlandischen Sprache, Hildesheim: Georg Olms Verlags Buchhandlung.

Klokeid, T.J.: 1970, 'Research on Mabuiag,' ms., MIT.

Kuno, Susumu: 1971, 'The Position of Locatives in Existential Sentences,' Linguistic Inquiry 2, 333-378.

Kuno, Susumu: 1973, The Structure of the Japanese Language, Cambridge, MA: MIT Press.

Kuno, Susumu: 1974, 'The Position of Relative Clauses and Conjunctions,' Linguistic Inquiry 5, 117-136.

Kuno, Susumu and J.J. Robinson: 1972, 'Multiple Wh Questions,' Linguistic Inquiry 3, 463-488.

Kuroda, S.-Y.: 1969, 'English Relativization and Certain Related Problems,' in Reibel and Schane (eds.).

Lakoff, G.P.: 1969, 'On Generative Semantics,' in D.D. Steinberg and Jacobovits, L.A. (eds.), Semantics, Cambridge, England: Cambridge University Press.

Lakoff, G.P.: 1974, 'Syntactic Amalgams,' in CLS 10, 321-344.

Lalou, Marcelle: 1950, Manuel Elementaire de Tibetain Classique, Paris: Imprimerie Nationale.

Lambton, A.K.S.: 1967, Persian Grammar, Cambridge, England: Cambridge University Press.

Lewis, G.L.: 1953, Teach Yourself Turkish, London: English Universities Press.

Lewis, G.L.: 1967, <u>Turkish</u> <u>Grammar</u>, London:   Oxford
    University Press.

Liberman, Mark: 1974, 'On Conditioning the Rule of Subject
    Aux Inversion,' in <u>NELS</u> <u>V</u>, 77-91.

Lockwood, W.B.: 1964, <u>An</u> <u>Introduction</u> <u>to</u> <u>Modern</u> <u>Faroese</u>,
    Copenhagen:   Munksgaard.

Loogman, Alfons: 1965, <u>Swahili</u> <u>Grammar</u> <u>and</u> <u>Syntax</u>,
    Pittsburg, PA:   Duquesne University Press.

Lowie, R.H.: 1941, <u>The</u> <u>Crow</u> <u>Language</u>, Berkely and Los
    Angelese, CA:   University of California Press.

Malisdorf, Zafrira: 1974, 'Relative Clauses in Hebrew,'
    ms., CUNY, New York.

Martin, L.W.: 1972, <u>Appositive</u> <u>and</u> <u>Restrictive</u> <u>Relative</u>
    <u>Clauses</u> <u>in</u> <u>English</u>, unpublished Ph.D. dissertation,
    University of Texas at Austin.

McCawley, J.D.: 1972, 'Japanese Relative Clauses,' in
    Peranteau, Levi and Phares (eds.).

McCawley, J.D.: 1973, 'External NPs versus Annotated Deep
    Structure,' <u>Linguistic</u> <u>Inquiry</u> 4, 221-240.

Meinhof, Karl: 1909, <u>Lehrbuch</u> <u>der</u> <u>Nama-Sprache</u>, Berlin:
    Druck und Verlag um Georg Reimer.

Montague, Richard: 1974, <u>Formal</u> <u>Philosophy</u>, New Haven,
    Connecticut:   Yale University Press.   Edited by
    Richard Thomason.

Peranteau, P.M, J.N. Levi and G.C. Phares, (eds.): 1972,
    <u>The</u> <u>Chicago</u> <u>Witch</u> <u>Hunt</u>, Chicago, IL:   Chicago
    Linguistic Society.

Perkins, Ellavina: 1975, 'Extrapostion of Relative Clauses
    in Navajo ,' <u>Diné</u> <u>Bizaad</u> <u>Nánil'įįh</u> (The Navajo
    Language Review) 2, Number 2.

Perlmutter, D.M.: 1970, 'On the Article in English,' in M. Bierwisch and K.E. Heidolph (eds.), Progress in Linguistics, The Hague: Mouton.

Perlmutter, D.M.: 1971, Deep and Surface Structure Constraints in Syntax, Holt, Rinehart and Winston.

Perlmutter, D.M.: 1972, 'Evidence for Shadow Pronouns in French Relativization,' in Peranteau, Levi and Phares (eds.).

Perlmutter, D.M. and J.R. Ross: 1970, 'Relative Clauses with Split Antecedents,' Linguistic Inquiry 1, 350.

Peters, Stanley: 1972, 'The Projection Problem: How is a Grammar to be Selected,' in Peters, Stanley (ed.), Goals of Linguistic Theory, Englewood Cliffs, NJ: Prentice-Hall.

Peters, Stanley and R.W. Ritchie: 1973, 'On the Generative Power of Transformational Grammars,' Information Sciences 6, 49-83.

Platero, P.P.: 1974, 'The Navajo Relative Clause,' International Journal of American Linguistics 40, 202-246.

Platero, P.R. and K.H. Hale: 1974, 'Aspects of Navajo Anaphora, Relativization and Pronominalization,' Diné Bizaad Nánil'įįh (The Navajo Language Review) 1, 9-25.

Postal, P.M.: 1971, Cross Over Phenomena, Holt, Rinehart and Winston.

Postal, P.M.: 1972, 'A Global Constraint on Pronominalization,' Linguistic Inquiry 3, 35-60.

Postal, P.M.: 1974, 'On Certain Ambiguities,' Linguistic Inquiry 5, 325-366.

Reibel, D.A. and S.A. Schane, (eds.): 1969, Modern Studies in English, Englewood Cliffs, NJ: Prentice-Hall.

Ross, J.R.: 1967, Constraints on Variables in Syntax, unpublished Ph.D. dissertation, MIT. Distributed by the Indiana University Linguistics Club.

Ross, J.R.: 1974, 'More on -er Globality,' Foundations of Language 12, 269-270.

Sapir, Edward: 1963, 'Abnormal Speech Forms in Nootka,' in D.G. Mandelbaum (ed.), Collected Writings of Edward Sapir, Berkely and Los Angeles, CA: University of California Press.

Satyanarayana, P. and K.V. Subbarao: 1973, 'Are Rightward Movement Rules Upward Bounded?,' Studies in the Linguistic Sciences 3, 183-192, University of Illinois.

Schultz-Lorentzen, C.W.: 1945, 'A Grammar of the West Greenlandic Language,' Meddelelser om Grönland 129, Copenhagen.

Selirk, Elisabeth: 1970, 'On the Determiner System of Noun Phrases and Adjective Phrases,' ms., MIT. Revised version published as Selkirk (1977).

Selkirk, Elisabeth: 1977, 'Some Remarks on Noun Phrase Structure,' in P. Culicover, T. Wasow and A. Akmajian (eds.), Formal Syntax, Academic Press.

Siegel, Dorothy: 1974, Topics in English Morphology, unpublished Ph.D. dissertation, MIT.

Soames, Scott: 1974, 'Rule Orderings, Obligatory Transformations, and Derivational Constraints,' Theoretical Linguistics 1, 116-138.

Southworth, F.C. and N.B. Kavadi: 1973, Spoken Marathi, Philadelphia, PA: University of Pennsylvania Press.

Stockwell, R., P. Schachter and B. Partee: 1973, The Major
Syntactic Structures of English, Holt, Rinehart and
Winston.

Thiersch, Craig: 1973, 'The Harder They Come, The Harder
They Fall,' ms., MIT.

Underhill, Robert: 1972, 'Turkish Participles,' Linguistic
Inquiry 3, 87-100.

Vergnaud, J.R.: 1974, French Relative Clauses, unpublished
Ph.D. dissertation, MIT.

Wackernagel, Jacob: 1930, Altindische Grammatik, Göttingen:
Vandenhoed und Ruprecht.

Wasow, Thomas: 1972, Anaphoric Relations in English,
unpublished Ph.D. dissertation, MIT.

Wilson, W.A.: 1963, 'Relative Constructions in Dagbani,'
Journal of West African Languages 1, 133-144.